To my Mum and Dad, Ted and Dora.

I like to think you're out there somewhere,
watching over us.

I talk to you, often.
I miss you.

Hoping *for a* Home

Janie Ritson

Hoping
for a
Home

How a woman with a big heart gave
new lives to animals in need

HARPER

HARPER

An Imprint of HarperCollins*Publishers*
77–85 Fulham Palace Road
Hammersmith, London W6 8JB

www.harpercollins.co.uk

First published in Great Britain by HarperCollins*Publishers* 2011

1 3 5 7 9 10 8 6 4 2

A catalogue record for this book is
available from the British Library

ISBN 978-0-00-737891-3

Printed and bound in Great Britain by
Clays Ltd, St Ives plc

Mixed Sources
Product group from well-managed
forests and other controlled sources
www.fsc.org Cert no. SW-COC-001806
© 1996 Forest Stewardship Council

FSC is a non-profit international organisation established to promote the
responsible management of the world's forests. Products carrying the FSC
label are independently certified to assure consumers that they come
from forests that are managed to meet the social, economic and
ecological needs of present and future generations.

Find out more about HarperCollins and the environment at
www.harpercollins.co.uk/green

Acknowledgements

Thanks to Anna and Marie Stevens, for giving me their blessing to feature them in this book, and to my family, who had no choice.

Authonomy: Thank you. Without you, there would be no book.

Preface

It all started when I was fourteen.

A neighbour found a featherless baby bird, and was going to kill it humanely. I asked him if I could have it. He laughed and said it would die, but gave it to me anyway.

I put it in a margarine tub, filled with cotton wool balls, and fed it on white bread and cow's milk (which is completely the wrong food for a baby bird). It grew feathers and cheeped at me. My dad told me it was a sparrow. I got an old budgie cage for it to live in, but it spent most of its time flying around my bedroom. My mum said I should release it back into the wild now that it was grown up, but at first I didn't want to.

Then one day, it sat on the windowsill and chirruped to a flock of sparrows in the garden. I felt sad, and took it downstairs and let it go. It flew straight to the flock and I watched for ages, with tears in my eyes, as it hopped around, being a proper sparrow for the first time in its life. When they flew off, it went with them.

Saving and rearing that little bird gave me a really good feeling.

From that moment, I wanted to work with animals, and when I was eighteen, got myself a job with chickens; eighty-eight thousand of them, in a battery farm. It was the summer of 1976, and loads of them died every day from the heat. I hated it. I felt so sorry for the chickens, cramped five to a tiny wire cage, that I let the sick ones out onto the floor. Within a week, about two hundred of them were loose. When my boss came in to check how I was doing, he saw them, went mad, and sacked me. As I was shown the door, I grabbed a particularly weak one and shoved her into my bag.

I called her Henrietta, and took her to the vet the next day. He said she had Marek's disease, which was why her legs were partially paralysed. He also said the mortality rate was high. She died four days later.

I haven't eaten meat since then.

I got a job looking after unwanted dogs in a boarding establishment, and it was my responsibility to get the dogs out for prospective owners to see. I absolutely loved it, and adopted two of the dogs, one of which had been in kennels for over five years.

I moved to Chichester, in West Sussex, married and had four daughters: Lisa, Kelley, Shanie and Edwina. The marriage didn't work out, but we parted very good friends.

I got a job looking after an elderly gentleman, and my mother looked after my girls.

Over the years, I had accumulated a number of unwanted animals, but even I had a limit, so when a neighbour asked me to take on her dog, I looked in the phone book for the number of the dog rescue people I'd got mine from. Instead,

I found a number for an RSPCA animal centre, just five miles away. The manager agreed to take the dog.

I got on well with the manager, became a volunteer driver for her, and collected unwanted animals if the owners didn't have their own transport.

Within days, I met Tony, the RSPCA Inspector, and fell head over heels in love. Fortunately, for me, it was reciprocated.

We were like chalk and cheese: I talked all the time, he said very little; I got quite emotional, he stayed calm; I loved animals unreservedly, he respected them. But we both loved reading, cigarettes and chocolate.

He was a regular visitor. When dealing with complaints, he would sometimes find that the people involved didn't want their pet any more, and were happy to sign it over to the RSPCA for re-homing. He would bring it into the centre. Very occasionally, he took the animal away from the owner, with or without consent, and prosecuted the owner. He was also responsible for rescuing sick or injured animals, and often spent hours trying to catch something that didn't want to be caught.

I couldn't help him with rescues during the day except when I had time off from the centre, but I went with Tony after work, whenever I could, as two pairs of hands were better than one. Our idea of an evening out was to battle through brambles, trying to grab a badger or fox that had been hit by a car.

After a year, the manager left, and I took over, and moved into the cosy cottage that went with the job. I met Anna, who'd worked at the centre before, and we clicked instantly.

I asked her to come back as my deputy, and she agreed. I had a lot to learn about how to run an animal centre, but RSPCA Headquarters ran a management training course which I attended.

RSPCA Headquarters is in Horsham, and is the national body responsible for all the RSPCA Inspectors throughout the country. They own some animal centres themselves, but most RSPCA animal centres are branch-owned and run by individual committees, as ours was. The primary aims were to ensure the smooth running of the centres and raise sufficient funds to keep them solvent.

When I moved from the area in 1990, I became a volunteer at my new, local animal centre, and when a vacancy for kennel assistant arose, I was offered the job. When the manager left, I applied for the position, and got it.

In 2004, Tony took early retirement. We had devoted our married lives to working for the RSPCA, so I made the decision to leave as well. I'd wanted to write for years, and had already written some stories about my time as manager at the previous animal centre, and so it was time.

We moved again, and now live in a little village in the Hampshire countryside, with our dogs, and can be found, most days, wandering around the Hundred Acre Woods.

CHAPTER 1

A New Hope for Titan

Four months into marriage and my stomach still lurched with love whenever my husband pulled up outside the old, wooden five-bar gate in his RSPCA van.

I ran and opened the gate as he reversed towards it, and I couldn't help my Cheshire cat grin as he slowly backed into the driveway. But Tony's face was unusually grim as he passed, and he offered me a ghost of a smile. Subdued, I closed the gate. Something was seriously wrong.

He walked straight into the office, sat on a hard-backed chair and leaned forward. With an enormous sigh he rested both elbows on his knees and his fingers took the weight of his forehead. I leaned over him and put my arms around his shoulders.

'What's wrong?' I whispered into his right ear. I moved back as he lifted his head and took my hands.

'I took a statement from a man today.'

I knelt in front of him, our hands still locked together.

'Why?'

'He hit his dog over the head with a shovel – hard.'

I took a sharp breath.

'Oh,' I whispered.

Tony gently moved me away from him and stood up, raising me with him. Letting go of one hand, he pulled me toward the back door of his van. He looked at me, such a sad look in his eyes, as he opened the door.

A Doberman stood there quietly, its back legs trembling as Tony untied the lead and coaxed it out of the van. He passed me the lead.

'Her name is Sophie. She's been examined by the vet and, physically, is fine. She's from the same home as the injured dog, possibly his mother, and is around seven years old.'

I talked quietly to Sophie as I walked her to an empty kennel, but she gave me no response. As the door clunked behind her, she flinched and dropped to the ground, quaking from head to foot.

Back at the van Tony had undone the lead on a second dog, this one lying flat, facing away from us, and smelling very strongly of antiseptic. My husband is a big man: over six feet tall, broad shoulders, not known for sentimentality; but watching him as he so very carefully manoeuvred the dog round to the door, I realised just how sensitive he actually is. Then I saw the dog's face, and understood why he was being so gentle. My eyes widened and both my hands went to my mouth as it opened in horror.

The dome-shaped head of this Doberman was caved in: but only on one side. A bright patchwork of stitches in orange-coloured thread adorned the badly swollen left side of his skull. A particularly neat row ran around the top of the eye socket, and down the side of his nose. His eyelids were slits in a mass of blue and purple bruising. With the fur

2

shaven off the injured side of his face and congealed blood stuck to his bare skin, he looked grotesque.

I dropped to my knees and spoke to him, touching the cheek on the undamaged but puffed up side of his face as I did so. He looked at me through his half closed good eye, then licked my hand with just the very tip of his tongue. Stumbling to my feet, I buried my head in Tony's chest, and sobbed.

Throughout my training I had been warned about this side of the job, but no amount of training could *ever* have prepared me for what now confronted me: the situation as a whole; not just what had happened to the dog but *why* it had happened. What made a human being decide to take a shovel and bash it over his pet dog's head with such force that the skull was not just cracked, but completely broken?

'His name is Titan,' Tony said as we carefully lowered the Doberman onto a blanket in a wheelbarrow. 'He's undergone extensive surgery, and the vet isn't sure if he will be permanently brain damaged as he hasn't used his legs since the operation. Only time will tell. He needs to be kept as quiet and isolated as possible.'

'The boarding block's empty and we don't have any dogs booked in for the next few days, so that's probably the best place for him. But Tony – he's not going in there on his own, I'm going to put Sophie in with him. They need each other.' I felt the tears prick my eyelids as I thought of Sophie, who, although apparently not physically hurt, was going through this too. Tony didn't argue.

Since Titan couldn't stand, I was concerned that if he tried to, he would fall and injure himself even more, so I removed the large, rigid dog bed from the kennel. Where the bed had been, I placed a pile of soft blankets that had been donated earlier that day on the floor, with a thick layer of newspaper in front of them. The dog was carefully laid down on the blankets, and once again he licked my hand. I sat down next to him and stroked his neck, talking to him as I did so, wondering why, after all this dog had been through, he *chose* to lick my hand. I didn't know how he could ever trust another human again.

Sophie was still trembling when I went to get her, but she stood quietly as I slipped a lead over her neck. Obediently, she followed me outside and round to the block that Titan was in. When she realised he was there, she whined excitedly to him. He turned his head at the noise but made no sound himself. He didn't move while Sophie sniffed his whole body and wagged her stump of a tail furiously; then, satisfied, she settled down next to him and went to sleep.

Sophie loved food, and quickly devoured everything that was put in front of her, but feeding Titan was a real issue. His head was so badly swollen and bruised that his mouth couldn't open properly, and he didn't even try to lap the milk that I put in front of him. He sniffed at whatever I offered him, then turned away and rested his head on the blanket. After a lengthy chat with the vet I went to the surgery to collect some 10ml syringes and sachets of Lectade, a powder that would help stop Titan from becoming dehydrated. Then to the shop to buy a liquidiser.

Chicken, boiled rice and the Lectade dissolved in water blended much better than I thought they would. This done, I cut the business end off one of the syringes, and pushed the hollow tube into the chicken mix. When I pulled the plunger I was childishly excited because it actually worked and the syringe was now full of food. I was eager to see how Titan would take to this method of eating.

Bless that dog, he didn't disappoint me. Once he tasted the food, he swallowed syringeful after syringeful, and got through the whole bowl of food. Sophie licked the bowl clean afterwards.

Tony took statements from the owner of Titan, the two vets who performed the operation on the dog, and the senior veterinary nurse who oversaw his post-operative care, and submitted them to RSPCA Headquarters for their consideration. Along with these were photographs: of the shovel used, with close-ups of the blood that had spattered onto it from Titan's skull; pools of his blood on the floor in the area where it had happened; and of Titan himself, showing the extent of his injuries before being operated on. These were particularly gruesome.

In the meantime, records had to be kept in case the RSPCA decided to go to court. Tony had already given me forms to fill in about everything that Titan ate, drank or did: any tablets that he had to take; and any progress that he made. Visits by the vet were also recorded, with the vet having to write down the details of his daily examinations, and then sign, date and even put the time of each visit. All very time-consuming and costly.

Now that Titan was eating, it was easy to crush his daily cocktail of antibiotic, anti-inflammatory and pain killing tablets into the food to be syringed into him. All we had to do now was get him on his feet again, if it was possible. The vet was still very concerned about whether Titan would walk again, and had asked us to massage his legs as often as we could to keep the blood circulating in them. But keeping the poor dog clean was also a problem. His bladder and bowels were working perfectly and he was messing where he lay, which was particularly unpleasant for him because he had diarrhoea and his back legs, sides and stomach were regularly covered in it. We were getting through numerous blankets every day, and the washing machine seemed to be permanently in motion. Outside, there were multi-coloured blankets hanging on the washing line and stretched over the wooden panel fencing – even over the bushes, in an effort to dry them. Eventually we decided to use some of the woollen clothing that had been donated, which we were then able to throw away when it was soiled.

I started getting up earlier to go and massage Titan's legs before work, and during the evenings Tony and I took it in turns. Even my nine-year-old daughter, Lisa, helped after school. She did one front leg while I did the other, at least she tried to, but Titan had other ideas, and would lick her so much that she had to stop and cuddle him while I continued to work on him. How could you not love this dog?

Anna, my deputy, took to having her tea break and lunch in the kennel with the dogs, where she would massage Titan's legs in between slurps of tea or bites of a sandwich. She discovered that Sophie loved to play with a ball, and before long she was leaving the kennel door open and throwing the ball outside for Sophie to chase after. Sophie would race across the grass, pick it up, and race back, dropping it straight into Anna's lap ready for the next time.

It was during one of these sessions that Anna screamed:
'JANE – JANE, QUICK – NOW – NOW, WOMAN!'

Dropping the bowl of dog food that I was preparing, I ran round to the kennel. And there was Titan standing by the door, peeing all over the ball Sophie had been playing with. He swayed a bit, and he didn't cock his leg, but he was standing. We watched, transfixed, as he finished his pee, then as he walked stiffly outside and on to the grass, where he pointed his nose upwards and sniffed the air. Anna and I looked at each other, and simultaneously burst into tears. Then we laughed hysterically while we cried, hugging each other with joy that Titan could walk. I went and made us a cup of tea to celebrate.

'Good news,' Tony told me and Anna a couple of days later. 'I had a letter from HQ today, saying they believe there is enough evidence to proceed with a case against Titan's owner. The dogs will be staying here until the case comes up.'

Anna immediately ranted about how she couldn't wait to see 'the bastard get his comeuppance'. We both agreed with her on that.

'What do you think is going to happen?' I asked Tony.

'We are going to ask for a lifetime ban on him keeping *any* dogs, as well as for both dogs to be signed over for re-homing, and for all costs to be reimbursed, which are very high because of the vet bills. The court will make a decision on the evidence that is presented to them. I think they will find him guilty, but the main thing is not getting the costs back, so much as getting the ban. If they don't ban him, he could get Titan and Sophie back ...'

That didn't bear thinking about.

The day came that Titan's stitches were to be removed, and we regarded it as a huge milestone in all our lives. The dog sat patiently on the office desk that had been cleared of paperwork and was now an examination table. He stoically accepted the vet's thorough examinination of his head. As I looked at Titan, I thought again how good-natured he was, and wondered for possibly the hundredth time how his owner could ever justify inflicting such an injury on him. Anna and I both shed a quiet tear as the last stitch came out, and we grinned at each other as we wiped them away with our sleeves.

The vet patted the dog's rump and told him what a good boy he was. Titan took this to mean he could go, and jumped down, shaking his entire body, right down to the tip of his four-inch tail. He had (unfortunately) come to know the surgeon quite well, and jumped up at him, his front legs draped over one of the man's arms. He was a bit of a gruff gent at times, but his eyes were glistening as he patted Titan on the neck. Satisfied, Titan trotted off with Sophie, who had been waiting patiently just outside the door.

I'm sure I caught the vet quickly wiping a hand across his face. I smiled to myself as I cleaned the desk off; this dog had got to all of us.

Titan, was, quite literally, coming on in leaps and bounds. He got to know Anna's dogs, who came with her to the centre every day and were an extremely sociable bunch. When they weren't sleeping, they would generally be found gambolling around with the two Dobermans in the hay store. Here the ground was covered with loose straw, and when stock was low enough, they could jump on and off the bales. I often got a lump in my throat when I watched them all playing together. Anna's dogs were so lucky, with not a care in the world; the future of the other two remained uncertain.

Over the following weeks, Titan and Sophie became part of life at the centre. Every morning the first thing Anna did was feed them, then open their kennel door. They were free to come and go as they pleased while we did the cleaning, then they shared biscuits and tea with us at break time. At eleven o'clock we opened to the public, so they went back into their kennel. One o'clock was lunch time, and out they came again. And so it went on.

Titan's fur had grown back quickly and the scars were barely visible unless you really studied his face. The only noticeable thing was the dip on top of his skull, which would be there for the rest of his life. He and Sophie were now both very happy, well-adjusted dogs. I wished that the wait for the court case could go on forever …

But, all too soon, the day arrived, and Tony dressed in his No. 1 uniform, fresh from the dry cleaners. He also spent ages doing 'spit and polish' on his black leather shoes, something he had been taught during his RAF service, and you really could see your face in the toe-caps. Armed with his briefcase full of documents, and the photos, I gave him a last quick hug as he went out to meet his Chief Inspector, who had been very interested in the case from the start, and who was going with him. He waved and blew me a kiss as they drove off. I wasn't a religious person – but I started praying before the van was out of sight. A look at my watch showed me it was only just gone nine in the morning: the beginning of one of the longest, least atheist days in my entire life.

It was gone five, and I had been almost hanging out of my front bedroom window for the last half an hour, watching and waiting for the Chief's van. Lisa kept me company. She had no idea about what had happened, or why the dogs were at the animal centre, but she knew that an important decision was being made about them that day, and told me that she had prayed for Titan during school assembly. When I asked her what she had prayed for, she answered, 'I asked God to make sure Titan never gets hurt again.'

If only it were that easy …

I'd had to give up waiting in the bedroom and was cooking the tea when I heard a car door slam.

At last.

My hands shook as I filled the kettle ready for Tony's coffee, and suddenly I was scared. *What if they had found the man not guilty? What if they had said he could have the dogs back? What if he was out there now – with Tony – waiting to take them?* My pulse raced as I tortured myself with 'what ifs'. Where the hell *was* Tony?

'Hello,' said Tony, as he closed the back door.

'Cut the crap – is he getting his dogs back?' I almost yelled at him, as the tension filling me spilled over.

'Well if you'll just give me a chance to speak, I'll tell you,' he replied, calm as ever.

'No, he's not.'

My legs gave way and I had to lean on the kitchen cupboard. My feeling of relief was indescribable, and the tears once more flowed, something that I had begun to get used to since working for the RSPCA. I was so glad my girls were busy playing in their rooms.

I had to ring Anna.

'Hello you old cow,' I said, using our mutual method of greeting. My voice did a stupid, high pitched wobble. 'It's okay. The dogs are OURS!'

Anna started screaming indecipherable words at me, but I gathered she was quite pleased. Once she had calmed down I continued.

'Tony hasn't told me anything yet except that, but I wanted to let you know straight away. Sweet dreams!'

I was so bursting with happiness at that moment that I wondered what a 'surge of emotion' felt like – I think I had just had one.

After our meal Tony filled me in with all the details. The owner was found guilty and fined several hundred pounds. He had been banned from keeping any dogs for ten years, and Titan and Sophie had now been signed over to us for re-homing. Tony was disappointed that it was only a ten-year ban, but we both agreed that it was better than no ban at all. Full costs had been awarded to the RSPCA.

Now we had to overcome the next challenge: re-homing them.

I opened the bedroom curtains the next morning, and was surprised to see several cars and vans parked along the edge of the road directly opposite.

'What on earth is going on? There are loads of cars parked outside, and men walking around with cameras – and one of the cameras is huge.'

I looked at Tony, who was sitting on the edge of the bed, fully expecting him to know the answer, and not surprised that he did.

'Ah. That'll probably be the press and TV. There was a lot of interest in the case yesterday, even a couple of national papers were there. They want to cover the story. Bit early though, aren't they?' he said, as he went to the bathroom, totally unperturbed.

A *bit* early. It was seven thirty in the morning.

Tony didn't rush, just went outside when he was ready; and once my girls were all packed off to school, I joined him. Anna was already there, parading Titan and Sophie around while photos were taken of them. I smiled, stood back, and started to enjoy the lack of the worry that had become such a burden over the last few weeks.

Anna was a natural, and as I watched her I realised how much I had come to look on her as a friend, not just as a deputy. She looked over at me, and winked as she posed kneeling between the two dogs, this time for the TV camera. They were licking her face ecstatically, and I knew that she wanted their banned owner to see this: to see how happy the dogs were, to give 'the bastard his comeuppance' personally – just from us.

We talked non-stop about the case and the cameras that day, not literally, but whenever we had the chance. And Anna rushed off that evening to catch the news, as we had been told that it would definitely be on both the early and the late news programmes. She was so excited, never having been on TV before.

Tony got us a Chinese take away to celebrate, and instead of sitting at the table, the girls sat on the floor in front of the

TV, and we sat on the sofa, and watched. When Anna appeared with the dogs, we all cheered, and for the first time, I *didn't* cry. It was just brilliant.

The next morning the phone rang constantly. No sooner had it been put down, than it rang again, and virtually all the calls were from people who had seen Titan and Sophie on the TV, and they wanted the dogs. It was completely over-whelming. We took the name and phone number of each person that called, and said we would phone them back. By lunch time, we'd had so many calls that I let the answering machine take them, to give us a chance to catch up.

Anna flopped down in the armchair and immediately disappeared under a sea of dogs. She struggled to get her head above them.

'Oh my God! What on earth are we going to do now? I can't believe so many people want the dogs. Sally – get your bum out of my face, I can't see.'

Sally was Anna's smallest dog, and she had a tendency to sit on Anna's head.

'Haven't a bloody clue,' I answered, lighting up a well earned cigarette. 'Ring them all back, take further details, and try to narrow it down until, well, I don't know. Christ, I never expected this to happen.' I leaned over the stable door of the office, and blew my smoke out into the air, still numb from the morning's events.

We slowly worked our way through the many numbers we had, and it didn't take long to realise that most of the callers only wanted the one dog – Titan. Of those that offered a home to both dogs, lots of them lived many miles away, and we thanked them but explained that we would be re-homing them within our own area. Others worked full time, and while we appreciated their generous offer, we told them that we always tried to put our animals into homes where the owners were not out regularly for more than four hours at a time, and thanked them for their call. This was mentally exhausting.

Then Mrs Hunt arrived.

'Hello, can I help you,' I asked the rather posh-looking woman who had just walked into the office.

'I hope so,' she replied. 'I had a message left on my answering machine about Titan and his companion. My name is Hunt, Jenny Hunt, how do you do.' Mrs Hunt proffered a hand.

'Ah! Hello, Mrs Hunt.' I moved toward her and shook her hand. 'Thank you for coming. I'm Jane, please take a seat.'

Mrs Hunt chose to sit on the edge of the armchair that was covered with Anna's dogs, which surprised me, considering the expensive-looking clothes she was wearing.

Over a cup of tea, we talked for a long time. I explained to Mrs Hunt what our requirements were for the two dogs; and she told me what she had to offer.

I liked Mrs Hunt. Now, we had to see what Titan and Sophie thought of her …

I took the dogs into an exercise run, where the lady was waiting. Initially, they sniffed her, then ran off to play. She didn't try and make them stay with her, instead she walked slowly along the fence, stopping here and there to look around. I hadn't seen anyone do this before; usually people called to the dog they were interested in to come to them, or followed the dog around, stroking it, and talking to it as they went. I was quite fascinated, and stayed to watch.

It was Sophie that first went to see what Mrs Hunt was up to, and she was rewarded with a small treat. Sophie was anyone's if food was involved, so it wasn't a surprise to see her following the woman around everywhere she went after that. And of course both dogs were attached, so it wasn't long before Titan was following too.

I thought it best to leave them to it for a while, and called over to Mrs Hunt to tell her. She smiled and nodded, then carried on with walking around. *Well,* I supposed to myself, *it's different anyway.*

Some time passed, and I went to see how the dogs were doing. I stopped half way down the track and watched as Mrs Hunt weaved around the exercise run at a trot, both dogs following on either side of her, with their heads almost glued to her hips, and no treats in sight. I was astonished.

'Jane!' said Mrs Hunt, as she laid a hand on each dog's head. 'I love them.'

I *really* liked Mrs Hunt.

The home check was going to be a formality, and was arranged for that afternoon. Tony was doing the check but I wanted – actually I *needed* to go and see where these dogs would be spending their lives, to satisfy myself that what was on offer was good enough for them.

If I died and came back as a dog – I would want to live with someone like Mrs Hunt. Not because she lived in a manor house and was remarkably well off, or because her landscaped garden of several acres contained lots of trees to pee up, and had a pond specially built for her dogs to play in, but because of the way she was with them.

Four Border Terriers greeted us when Tony pressed the button on the ancient, lichen-covered brick wall that held up the wrought iron gates at the main entrance. But immediately they flew back to Mrs Hunt when she called them, and crowded around her, so full of happiness and exuberance, and jumping around her like yoyos. In return, she put her hands down to them, often, just to touch their heads.

We were swept in through the huge, solid oak front door, and taken on a tour of where the dogs would eat, play, and sleep. Somewhere along the line, we came across Mr Hunt, who joined us. When we got to the kitchen, he stopped to organise refreshments while we continued the tour through the house with Mrs Hunt. Eventually we went out of a back door into the beautiful garden, where Mr Hunt was already seated, with a brew of strange-smelling tea and Battenberg cake ready for us. I looked around me as I listened to the banter between husband and wife, and the pretend scolding of one of the dogs, who had just helped itself to a piece of cake from Mr Hunt's plate, and I pictured Titan and Sophie here. Yes. Tony caught my eye and winked at me.

Mr and Mrs Hunt visited every day for the next week, bringing their Terriers with them, and we watched as Titan and Sophie became more and more attached to their new family. Finally, with the adoption forms filled in and signed, the couple stood waiting, with two new, black leather leads, and collars to match, each with a name engraved on a silvery metal plate.

Titan
Sophie

I hadn't cried for a while, so I supposed it wouldn't hurt to get emotional now. After all, although they would only be in the next village, I didn't know when, or even if, I would see them again. Mrs Hunt gave me a tissue, and then gave one to Anna, who was also crying as she brought the dogs to us.

'I promise to keep in touch, dears, in fact, from now on, I shall pop in to buy treats for them regularly,' said Mrs Hunt, as she looked around at the shelves full of dog and cat food, treats and toys.

And she did.

That December, I stood in the office, all excited as I opened what looked liked my first Christmas card. It was from Mrs Hunt, and showed the Dobermans lying asleep together in front of a beautiful, real log fire. Decorations and holly adorned the fire place, and hanging either side of the blazing fire were two stockings which bore the names Titan and Sophie.

CHAPTER 2

River Rescue

'Hello there, Tony!' said Dave, the RSPCA Inspector on weekend phone duty. 'I'm really sorry about this mate, but there's a sheep caught up in barbed wire. We don't know who the owner is; would you be able to attend?'

'You knew I was just about to sit down to my roast dinner, didn't you, Dave?' responded Tony, with a bit of a sigh.

'Now Tony – you know me better than that! I'm the last person to want to drag you away from your dinner and send you a good twenty miles over to Storrington, especially on a cold, wet and windy November day. Roast beef is it? With Yorkshire pudding?'

'No. Lamb, with mint sauce.'

'Ah, appropriate that it's a sheep rescue calling you away from it then, methinks,' laughed Dave. 'And the distance is the good news, old lad; the bad news is that you will have to walk about half a mile along a footpath, and the sheep is hanging over the bank of the river.'

'Christ,' said Tony, 'give me the rest of the details on the van radio, will you? I'll get out there as quickly as possible. Oh – and I'm on phone duty in a couple of weeks, I'll see if I can give you a nice little errand in the pouring rain …' He was already gathering his keys and diary.

'Put mine in the oven will you, love? I have to go out'.

'Hang on – I'm coming too.' I manoeuvred his large oval plate onto the top shelf of the oven. My much smaller, vegetarian plate was piled high with roast potatoes which I was loath to leave, but begrudgingly I closed the oven door and went to the hall to grab my coat. As I put my arms into the sleeves I looked out at the rain beating against the window, and shivered involuntarily.

The van was parked about three hundred feet away, by the main gate, so we dashed off through puddles that had already formed on the tarmac. As I put on my seat belt and settled down, I realised I was quite breathless.

'Must stop smoking,' I muttered to myself more than to Tony, as I got my cigarettes out of my pocket and lit two, handing one to him. But not now though.

Dave had only given us the bad news: the worse news was that the footpath was no longer. It was an ex-footpath, now a lethal combination of fast-running water, slippery leaves and thick mud.

Completely sodden and weighed down with half a ton of the mud on our wellies, we finally reached the sheep, which was now dangling over the edge of the bank, just a couple of feet above the raging torrent of water that was normally a gentle flowing river.

'Oh shit …' was both our responses.

'Right.' Tony sat down on the saturated bank and shouted over the sound of rain and river. 'The safest way to get her back up is to sit either side of her.'

I straight away sat on the other side of her.

'Ok, have you got something to hang on to? A sturdy bush or …'

'Yes! – yes, I'm hanging on to something,' I shouted back impatiently. Tony put a lot of thought into whatever he did – even the best thing to hang on to whilst sitting in mud.

We got hold of her wool, and heaved.

Slowly, we hauled her up the side of the bank. But the barbed wire of the fallen fence kept snagging on the foliage, and just when I was beginning to feel relieved that we were almost there, the fence post that the wire was attached to snapped and toppled down toward the river, pulling the wire that was wrapped around the sheep taut. She wasn't going anywhere.

'Sod it,' Tony swore, 'I'll have to cut her loose now, will you be okay holding?'

My fingers were stiff with the cold, but they were twisted tight through her long wool.

'Yes, I'll be fine, go for it.'

As he cut the wire, it pinged away into the stinging nettles, and with the tension released the sheep suddenly came to life and struggled to get up the last bit of bank. Instead, she slid back down.

'TONY! I'M LOSING HER …' I screamed, as her weight became too much for my numb fingers, and I felt her slipping away.

He lunged forward and managed to grab one of her front legs.

'Jesus; that was close,' I mumbled, as we pulled her up the last bit of bank to safety.

We both just sat for a while, needing time to get over our experience, and I managed to light a cigarette under my coat. But I offered it to Tony first, and the end was extinguished by the heavy rain before it even reached him. He grinned at me.

'Come on, the sooner we do this, the sooner we get home to our dinner. Get a hold of her and I'll start cutting.'

She was well and truly entangled, not only in barbed wire but also brambles, big ones, which were covered in those huge thorns that rip your skin as if it's tissue paper. Both of us found it difficult to work with gloves on in a situation like this, and chose to suffer instead.

Rain lashed sideways at us, getting in our eyes and making it difficult to see what we were doing, but eventually, taking it in turns to cut and hold, we removed most of the brambles. The sheep was exhausted, and when I could I stroked her cheeks and muttered reassuring words to her. She kept her head high and her eyes closed.

The barbed wire was much worse to cut through. With all the thrashing around that she must have done, it was deeply embedded, and the skin between her front legs was bloodstained. Slowly, methodically, we followed it through her thick wool, teasing it away from her skin and cutting it off, bit by bit. It took an eternity.

Underneath the bloodstained wool, her skin hung in shreds, and blood, mud, and rain, dripped from her onto the churned up ground below her. She tried to make another feeble dash for freedom, but collapsed in a heap on the ground.

We were wet through and frozen, and I wanted nothing more than to go home to our nice cosy cottage, and sit in front of our nice cosy fire with my dinner on my lap, and watch one of the old black and white films that I loved, but the sheep was clearly injured so we couldn't just walk away and leave her. Tony tried to coax her to her feet, but we could see it wasn't going to work. We didn't speak: there was no need; we knew what had to be done – she would have to be carried. Tony took hold of her back end, which was unfortunate, because it was covered in runny shit, and I took her front, and between us we slithered slowly along the flooded track.

Only once did we slip over. Tony landed on his backside and the sheep thudded into his chest, winding him badly. I somehow went over the top of them both, and landed on my hands and knees, but because it was so slippery my hands just kept going and my sleeves filled with mud as I tried to stop short of my face going in it.

Great.

But we recovered our composure, Tony recovered his breath, I emptied my sleeves, and in as dignified a manner as possible, we continued on our way.

At first, I talked to the sheep, trying to make her less frightened, but the going was hard, and she seemed to have totally withdrawn. I felt so sorry for her, she was hurting and being hauled through mud by a couple of strange humans; it couldn't have been worse. She gave the occasional grunt, and kept her eyes shut, but eventually, she did rest her head on my arm. I squeezed her a little tighter and whispered to her that she was going to be okay, but my efforts to comfort her were becoming weaker, as were my limbs, so I slowly became silent, immersed in my own pain and discomfort.

As we slowly trudged along I looked around me. It was now dusk, and dark silhouettes of trees loomed over us, dripping huge raindrops down the backs of our necks even though it had stopped raining. I could barely see the path now. Where it ran right alongside the bank of the river each step had to be taken carefully because you couldn't always see where it was. Listening intently helped a bit.

Oh God – this is hell …

I thought about how we both loved our respective jobs, and the satisfaction we always felt when we had achieved what we set out to do, but this – this was just plain depressing. I only kept going because I had to: because this sheep, which was getting heavier, had to see a vet; because I wanted to go home …

It was pitch black and pouring again when we finally made it to the van.

Tony always carried blankets and towels with him, so we wrapped them round the shaking, very-poor sheep, and wedged some towels under her chin.

Sitting, at last, towelling our hair, we spoke for the first time in hours.

'My cigarettes are bloody wet through,' I said, dismally. 'Even the packet has fallen apart.'

Tony handed me one from the glove box. We drove off in silence.

Tony radioed Dave, and Dave called a vet, who made a point of saying that he hoped we realised he was going to be dragged away from his dinner.

Well, that makes three of us.

He met us at his surgery, and said not a word when we carried the sheep through his pristine waiting room: bedraggled, dripping, and covered in sheep shit. He simply opened the treatment room door and we laid our burden on the bench. She was now steaming because she had warmed up nicely in the van.

'I had absolutely no idea, I do apologise,' he said, looking us up and down.

He must be feeling guilty about the dinner comment then …

'Please, go home now, I'll call my nurse. You're soaked through and you will be ill if you stay like that.'

He was already examining the sheep's chest.

'Dear God, this is a mess. Barbed wire is a bloody awful thing. General anaesthetic required I'm afraid. Off you go now, you've done all you can.' He ushered us to the door as he spoke. 'Phone my receptionist in the morning to arrange collection. Check-up in three days, stitches out in ten.' He always talked in a staccato voice.

I looked back at the sheep as we walked away, and she looked at me, and I felt an affinity with her. We had been through hell that afternoon, all of us, but now she was safe. I had already decided that if no one phoned about her, I would keep her, and had even chosen a name: Barbie.

The thought of going home at last was quite cheering. I glanced sideways at Tony as we drove. 'At least we've built up a good appetite for our dinner now.'

'Oh, yes! I've thought about my roast a few times: tender lamb, home made mint sauce, lashings of gravy smothering honey-roast parsnips …'

'Mmm, sprouts, carrot and swede all mashed up with butter and black pepper, broad beans and mountains of roast potatoes covered in onion gravy ...' We lapsed into silence as we envisaged the dinners that awaited us.

Showered, and in warm dry clothes, Tony headed for the office to let Dave know what had happened, while I went to the kitchen to put the kettle on and prepare his coffee. Then I turned towards the oven. The door was open and the plates were ... empty – except for one small, lonely sprout.

NO! They can't be gone, they can't be ...

They were.

I stood in the middle of the kitchen, bewildered, as I remembered the last glimpse of my roast potatoes as I'd closed the oven door on them earlier. But as Tina, my elderly Collie cross, walked in, I knew immediately where the dinner had gone. Her rib cage was distended, her belly huge – and she still had a bit of mashed carrot stuck on the top of her nose.

'Oh Tina! How could you! And how did you open the door? Oh! You greedy bitch you – and why did you leave one sprout?' I said dismally.

Tony came in. 'Dave was very amused when I told him how I got winded by a sheep. I'm really looking forward to this, I'm so hungry now. Where's my dinner?'

I cringed as he stared at his plate.

'The dinner, where's the dinner?' He looked bewildered now. Then he looked at Tina, who stood between us. She looked up at him with her beautiful, soft brown eyes, and belched pleasurably ...

'Tony, I'm so sorry. The dinner's not in the oven any more because – well, the dinner's in the dog ...'

CHAPTER 3

Feline Frightened!

'Arghh!'

Tony came rushing over to the hay store. 'What on earth is the matter?' he shouted, on seeing me rooted to the spot.

'It leapt at me!' I gasped. 'Just launched itself and flew at me …'

'What did?' Tony asked, amusement written all over his face.

'I don't know. As I pulled down a bale of hay, a … beast came with it.' My voice trembled with shock.

He laughed at me quite openly so I gave him one of my best 'disgusted' looks.

'Don't laugh at me!' I shrieked almost hysterically, 'it's NOT FUNNY. It was huge, I tell you – and it leapt onto my shoulder.' I was already searching my skin for any marks to prove that I had actually been attacked. 'There!' I said triumphantly, and showed him two scratches, each about an inch long and oozing blood.

'Oh Janie,' he said, as he cupped my face lovingly in his hands, 'I do love you. Come on. I'll get some antiseptic from my first aid box.'

Still shaking, I let him take my arm and lead me to the office which was also the staff room. An ancient brown leather armchair nestled in one of the corners, and was often draped with Anna's snoozing dogs. Anna, my deputy, owned the dogs, and they thought they owned the chair. There were four of them sprawled over it when we entered, so I slid carefully on to the edge in an effort not to disturb them, nevertheless several eyes opened lazily and grunts of disapproval were uttered, before they got back to the serious business of sleeping.

As I daubed cream onto my scratches, my thoughts turned to rabies, and I wondered for just a second or two if it could be contracted without actually being bitten. When I mentioned my concern to Tony he smiled benevolently at me, and pointed out that the UK was rabies free.

One strong cup of tea later I felt much improved, and allowed the incident to drift to the back of my mind.

I kept away from the hay store for a couple of days, but increasingly often thought about the beast. *What the hell was it? Had it meant to attack me? Was it still here? Had it happened …?* Curiosity finally got the better of me.

I stood quietly next to the entrance, and leaning forward, peeked in. The store was fairly small, with no windows, and one slightly-wider-than-average doorway. It was quite dark in the corners. About thirty bales of hay and straw were stacked against the back wall, four high mostly, but there was a small gap between two at the top. I crept quietly towards it, and reaching up, carefully wrapped my fingers round the binder twine on one of the bales.

'I'm not scared this time, you bloody beast,' I whispered between gritted teeth, my heart beating fast. Holding my breath, I pulled the bale toward me, moving quickly aside as it landed on the floor next to me with a dull thud.

Motionless, I waited. Nothing leapt at me: there was silence. I watched as dust billowed in the air around me. Then I saw her, laying stretched out on her side, and squirming around between her legs were three tiny, newborn kittens, one of them still quite wet. My stomach lurched as I took in the sight before me.

My 'beast' was a scrawny-looking cat with badly torn ears and weeping sores all over her body. There was little fur left to show that she was a grey tabby, with hip bones and spine protruding offensively through her skin. In the dim light her one redeeming feature was visible: her eyes – big, beautiful, and emerald green. I put my hand up to her, but her ears went flat down on her head and a growl issued from way down in her throat. Then she yowled, straining at the same time, and I realised another kitten was on the way. The fact that she was even alive, I found amazing; that she had the strength to give birth to a litter of kittens was incredible. My eyes filled with tears as I watched her strain. Meowing pitifully, she pushed the fourth kitten into the world.

With my vision still blurred, I went to the kitchen, put the kettle on, and opened up a new tin of Cimicat, a powdered milk formula specially prepared for pregnant and lactating cats and orphaned kittens. I made milk for her and tea for me. The vet's advice for feeding an emaciated animal was 'little and often', so armed with a small amount of roast chicken which had been defrosting for my old dog, and the milk, I made my way back to the hay store.

The fourth kitten still hadn't been cleaned, but had found its way to the teats and now searched for milk, but with umbilical cord and placenta still attached and trailing behind, its progress was being seriously hindered. I took the large pair of scissors which were always wedged in a hole at the top of the door frame, ready for cutting the twine on the bales, and carefully snipped the cord as far away from the kitten as I could, then using the scissors as tweezers I closed them slowly on the placenta and managed to remove it without making too much mess. The exhausted cat watched me as I worked but didn't move until I placed the bowls of food and milk in front of her. Then she sat up straight and growled at me as she pressed herself back against a bale behind her. However, the smell of warm roast chicken got the better of her, and hunger overcame her fear as she came towards the bowl, devoured the chicken in seconds, and then lapped furiously at the milk until that too was all gone.

Then something surprised me. With eyes closed, and appearing relaxed for the first time since I had seen her, she purred a gentle, rhythmic purr and her front paws pummelled at the air. I wept as I watched her, because despite the state she was in, even with the suffering she had so obviously endured – was still enduring – she was content.

I watched and fed her throughout the day, and it appeared that her kittens, all black and white, were getting enough milk from her because they suckled periodically and remained settled. At about eleven o'clock that evening I paid my last visit for the day, and found them all sleeping soundly.

I silently prayed that the kittens would still be there, and alive, the next morning.

That evening I told Tony about my 'beast'. We both laughed about it, and I admitted to feeling stupid when the beast turned out to be a cat. It wasn't the first time something like this had happened. When we had only been living at the animal centre for a few weeks I had already been badly frightened by strange noises in the night.

One night, with children and, unusually, all dogs asleep, the whole place was silent. Tony, not only my new husband, but also the RSPCA Inspector for that area, had been called out to an injured badger. It was nearly midnight and one of my favourite pastimes was looking at the stars, so with a mug of strong tea and a fleece blanket to keep out the chilly April night, I went out into the front garden. The sky was cloudless, and because there were no street lights around for miles, the stars were particularly bright. I lay back on a reclining garden chair, stared up at the sky, and sighed with deep and utter contentment.

Then I heard a strange noise. It seemed far away, and for a while I listened, wondering idly as I puffed at my Lambert & Butler what was making it. Even though it was quite eerie I wasn't too bothered about it, and continued admiring the night sky.

Time passed peacefully, then the noise came again, only this time much closer. I sat up, stiff and straight, and the hairs on the back of my neck stood on end. I listened intently, but the minutes passed without another sound. I reclined again, the hairs went back down, and I continued to count my blessings.

ARRGHRRGGHH UPRRGHH

I fell sideways off my recliner, spilling the last of the tea down my jeans, and sat on the grass with a plop.

ARRGHRRGGHH UPRRGHH

Heart beating wildly, I raced across the grass and threw myself at the door, slamming it shut behind me.

Deep breath – deep breath, calm down.

With legs feeling like jelly I made my way to the living room.

Prioritising: another cigarette, deeply inhaled, was followed by closing the curtains and leaving no gaps – anywhere – then turning the TV up very loud. Then I didn't move.

'Why is the TV so loud?' shouted Tony when he came home some time later. I jabbered on about what had happened.

To be fair to him, he didn't smile until I said the noise sounded like an old man dying, when I had expected him to laugh about me falling off the chair. But he only smiled.

'Do you want me to go outside and look around?' he offered.

'No: thanks, but whatever it was must have gone by now. I just want to go to bed.'

Calling my dogs, I took myself off up the winding staircase, stopping half way to close a curtain at a tiny leaded window. Just before doing so, I cupped my hands onto the glass and pressed my forehead onto them. Blackness. Nothing to see out there but blackness. The stars had gone. I lay awake for ages that night unable to get 'the noise' out of my head.

Several weeks later I found out what 'the noise' was. Walking my dogs in the field next to the animal centre, I spotted a herd of deer in the distance. They hadn't noticed us and were grazing quietly, so I crouched down and called my dogs to me, and we sat there while I watched the herd move slowly along as they ate. I counted nine of them altogether, and they were the most beautiful wild creatures I had ever seen. Then a stag, with an enormous set of the most magnificent antlers, lifted his head high:

ARRGRRGGHH UPHRRHH!

I had heard the sound often since then. This new 'beast' that had scared me half to death now gave me another sleepless night, as I constantly wondered if she would still be there in the morning. By six o'clock I couldn't stay in bed any longer, and crept quietly down the stairs. My ankle-length, red dressing gown looked odd with my steel toe-capped wellingtons poking out from underneath. I picked up some fresh food and milk. With a torch to light the way, I felt a bit like Wee Willy Winkie, and giggled quietly to myself, then, quiet, I entered the store with trepidation.

Shining the torch slightly to the side of where the cat had been the day before, I heaved a sigh of relief. She was still there, and all the kittens were alive. She growled at me again, but then stood up and stretched before going to the food bowl that I had just placed in front of her. She ate more slowly this time, but watched me continuously. She was not going to trust me in a hurry.

It was a Saturday, and very busy, so I had little time to spend with my beast. Having provided enough food and milk to last her for several hours, I didn't get back over to see her until the centre closed at four o'clock, then with a bowl of tinned rabbit and game, water and milk, I called to her as I reached the doorway.

She wasn't there.

Instead, I looked into the menacingly dark eyes of an ugly, black and white cat, and gawped.

What? … WHAT! Where is she? WHO ARE YOU?

The cat emitted a continuous growl, broken only by spurts of spitting, and swiping at me with a paw. Ears down flat, head cocked sideways, mouth open wide exposing its sharp canine teeth, body tense – this cat was going to spring at me any second.

I backed off quickly, stunned, and perched on an upside-down bucket to think.

It's the same colour as the kittens. It appeared at the same time as the tabby. It's got to be the father. Probably. I didn't know, but to my mind, that was the only explanation.

I stood slowly, not wanting to disturb this ugliest of cats, and glanced over towards it. Tufts of chocolaty black and grubby white fur stuck out all over its body, and it too was covered in sores, like my beast. The tail looked as if it had been broken somewhen, with the last three inches or so hanging at an odd angle. Its left ear looked as if someone had taken scissors to the tip, and a good third was missing. A pot belly hanging below a skeletal frame suggested that it was riddled with worms too.

Remember to crush worm tablets into the next bowl of food, but first, remember to check with the vet to make sure the beast can be wormed too.

The ugly cat was more interested in drinking than eating, and quickly lapped up the bowlful of milk, but warned me often not to go any closer.

I wandered away, deep in thought, and worried.

It was two more hours before the beast came back, and although she brought with her a dead young rabbit, she was ravenous. She didn't see me sitting in a dark corner as she leapt up to her kittens, carrying the rabbit carcass up with her. There she went straight to the food. After giving them a perfunctory sniff, the chunks of tuna and pilchard were quickly demolished. Meanwhile the kittens all woke up and mewed as they crawled around searching for milk.

But when the bowl of food was empty, my beast stared directly at me, the look lasting for several seconds, before turning to her mate – she rubbed a cheek along the side of its face, purring loudly – then wrapping herself around her babies and going to sleep.

The ugly cat had eaten, but it grabbed the dead rabbit aggressively and climbed up onto the highest bale of hay, where it proceeded to crunch on bone. My stomach churned at the thought of what part it was eating, and I left.

As soon as my alarm went off the next morning I shot out of bed and rushed off to see the cats, not even bothering to get fresh food for them this time. Reaching the doorway I called quietly to them as always, then slowly made my way towards them.

The cats were lying, heads touching, bottoms facing away from each other forming a sort of arc with their bodies, and in between them, kittens galore squirmed.

WOW!

TWO MUMS!!

I stood there for ages, beaming at them all as the kittens blindly climbed over each other in their search for milk. The new litter were all tabbies, and eventually I decided that there were seven of them. Both litters were well and truly mixed up and suckling from both cats, and both mums were randomly licking each other's, as well as their own young.

I quickly got fresh food and milk, and they licked the bowls clean. When they lay back down together, they almost surrounded the kittens. I lost all track of time as I watched them licking, first their own paws, and then each other's faces, and the kittens wriggled from teat to teat until they were sated.

Eventually all movement stopped, and the only noise that broke the silence was the booming purr of both cats. Well, so much for my theory that the ugly cat was the father of the first litter …

I left them in peace.

It became obvious over the next few days that the cats were definitely feral. They watched and waited until they thought no-one was around before slinking away into the bushes, and if they were caught by surprise, they scrambled up the side of the wall and onto the roof, where they sat patiently waiting until the coast was clear. Once, the ugly cat even darted between my legs to escape. Never did they leave the kittens alone while they were young. If I tried to stroke one of the mums, they growled, hissed and spat at me. The beast smacked the back of my hand and caught three of her claws in my skin, which she promptly ripped off, leaving me with three very sore wounds. I wasn't going to try that again in a hurry.

Over a period of time I moved the food bowls further away, until the cats were eating just inside the cattery door, which luckily was right next to the hay store. They had both begun to put on weight, and their fur was growing nicely, but they still had sores on their bodies. Worse was the fact that I had recently noticed bald patches on two of the kittens as well. I had to catch them, and get them treated.

It wasn't until the kittens were about four weeks old that they were left by both mums for the first time. I seized the opportunity. The kittens had become used to me and were tolerant of my visits, but they turned into little furry balls of hiss and spit when I tried to pick them up. Luckily, this was amusing rather than painful. I placed them into the bed section of the first unit just inside the door of the cattery and left them a bowl of cooked chicken. Pushing the food bowl for the mums further into the corridor than usual, I sat quietly out of sight on an old milking stool, and waited.

An age later, the cats came back, trotted happily into the cattery and made straight for the food. I had already tied a piece of string to the door handle, which I pulled gently – and that was that. They were in. I have never, ever caught feral cats so easily since.

The veterinary practice advised me that I would need to take one of the cats to the surgery for skin scrapings to be taken, which meant a general anaesthetic for the unlucky cat. The dilemma now was choosing which one.

'Eenie meenie minee mo …' The ugly cat drew the short straw.

A grasper is a hollow metal pole approximately three feet long, with plastic coated wire running through it. The wire is made into a handle for pulling at one end, and a noose that can be pulled tight once around an animal's neck at the other end. Although I had been trained, I'd never used one on my own before, and my confidence in my ability was nil.

Gravity means nothing to a cornered feral cat. And this one was doing absolutely everything to avoid being caught with the grasper. She leapt up the wall, used the ceiling as a springboard then flung herself at the opposite wall, where she touched down for a split second before launching herself again and landing on the floor right in front of me – then she started all over again. It was like watching an out of control ping pong ball.

Eventually she stopped, and after allowing her to calm down for a while, I gently lowered the grasper towards her, talking quietly to her all time. Just as the noose reached her head, she sprung into action again, this time running clockwise around the edge of the unit. As I tried to intercept her with the grasper I trod on the side of one of the litter trays, which catapulted granules of grey cat litter all over my legs, along with several bowel actions that the kittens had previously produced. Blobs of poo stuck to my jeans, and time stood still as I watched one roll slowly down, and settle on the lace of my trainer. This was such fun …

Again, ugly cat finally stopped, panting heavily now.

I tried to take advantage of her tiredness, and bent slowly to slip the noose gently over her head, but her neck disappeared, and her head somehow lay flat against her shoulders, giving me nothing to hook it over.

A stroke of luck: as I enlarged the noose in front of her, she leapt through it, and landed in the cage I had ready for her on the floor. With a huge sigh of relief, I grabbed the lid and closed it on her. In less than an hour the beast was anaesthetised and being examined …

Ringworm! They both had ringworm, but the vet assured me it was treatable. And it was. Within a couple of weeks the sores disappeared and fur began to cover the bald patches. The two kittens with sores were also treated, and eventually all eleven of them were successfully re-homed despite still being a little nervous with humans.

With all the kittens gone, the beast and the ugly cat were spayed and released at the animal centre, and were forever afterwards known as – Beast and Ugly Cat.

I was scratching a really itchy area on my left shoulder and it felt strange, like a raised circle.

'Anna, have a look at my shoulder would you,' I asked my deputy, 'it really itches.'

'Hmm, never seen one of those before. That's weird; I think you should see a Doctor.'

I made an appointment for later that day.

'Do you work with animals?' my Doctor asked me.

'Yes, actually I do.'

'I thought so. You've got ringworm …'

* * *

Just in case anyone wonders what happened to the cats, I took them with me when I moved, and they became tame enough, over the years, for me to stroke.

When they were spayed the vet estimated their ages at approximately four to five years. In 2002, I found Beast under the pear tree at the bottom of our garden, curled in a ball. It looked as though she had died in her sleep.

Ugly Cat died in early 2003, in her cat bed, in our kitchen. They were both around seventeen years old.

CHAPTER 4

Who's a Pretty Boy?

My mother never shouted between the hours of eleven and four because, except for lunch time, the animal centre was open to the public, but today she was in full cry and it was only twelve o'clock. 'Stop it. STOP IT! Bloody dogs. GET IN. GET OUT! Ooooh …'

I had the best mum. She was a grey-haired, roly-poly sort of mum, who lived in polyester cardigans and crimplene dresses. Now retired, she travelled sixteen miles every day just to look after my daughters while I worked. Our unruly dogs were also part of the package, and at that moment it sounded like they were having one of their 'nearly' fights, where they nearly bit each other, but not quite.

I ran from the office and once indoors followed the snapping and snarling noises through the kitchen into the dining room. The culprits – my Collie cross, Tina, and Tony's German Shepherd, April – stopped as soon as they saw me, and slunk off in different directions. They had disliked each other since the day we all moved in together and these episodes were frequent.

'You okay, Mum?'

'Yes love, I'm fine. Sorry I shouted, but I thought they were going to bite each other this time. They really are getting worse. I'm more worried about them hurting one of the kids than anything else though.'

I was worried too. They had knocked over Edwina, my two-year-old, several times during their spats. Not that Edwina minded; she slept with them in front of the gas fire, using them as pillows, shared her chocolate, crisps and bottles of tea with them, and chattered to them incessantly while tucking blankets around them, pretending they were her babies. The Irish Wolfhound was twice her height. She was amused when they fought too. 'They shout like Mummy and Tony do …'

My mind was troubled as I made my way back to the office.

'I heard the ruckus. There's a cuppa on the fireplace,' said Anna, who was trying to put together what looked like a parrot stand.

'Thanks, Anna. If they don't end up killing each other, I'm sure I'll do it for them.' Sighing, I walked over to her. 'What is it and why are you putting it together?'

She replied through a mouthful of bolts, 'It's for the parrot that Tony's got in his van.'

'Not in the van any more,' he said as he walked in with the bird sitting quite happily on his shoulder.

Anna spat the bolts out, 'Aharr! All ye need now is an eye patch and a wooden leg, eh, me hearty!'

I rushed to the door and closed it. 'What are you doing?! It could have flown off and then what!'

'Don't worry, he can't fly – look.' Tony took the end of one of the wings and pulled it out to show us the feathers, or lack of, as there were only three.

'Oh,' said Anna. 'What happened to all his breast feathers too? It looks like he's been plucked.'

Now we could see the parrot resembled an oven-ready chicken, except for one little yellow feather which was growing upside down and to the left of his breast bone, and some tiny blue veins running across his skin.

'He pulls the feathers out himself, been doing it for years apparently. His name is Bertie, and he's a Blue and Gold Macaw. He likes listening to music so the owner has given us a radio to keep him company when he's on his own.' Tony scratched the bird's head as he spoke. Bertie crooned back at him then pulled at his earlobe, very gently.

Anna and I looked at each other – she had a hand over her mouth and was stopping herself from laughing, but a small snigger escaped from me. Oblivious, Tony perched on the desk and talked to the bird, still scratching its head. He was well rewarded. 'Brrr, brrr, pretty boy, preeetty boy,' said the parrot as it slowly pulled a large thread in Tony's jumper with its beak.

It was too much – we burst out laughing. Anna got hold of Tony's other sleeve, 'Pretty boy, preeetty boy!' She pulled at the sleeve, pretending to undo a thread.

It took us quite a while to finish the stand.

Within a couple of days I knew that Bertie didn't like me. No matter how much I tried, no matter how many nuts or pieces of fruit I hand fed him, he still attacked me at every opportunity. Tony found it very amusing until the day I wasn't quick enough and Bertie got hold of my thumb. With his big, powerful beak he squeezed …

In immense pain and unable to move, I watched as my nail parted company with the skin underneath. Specks of blood oozed and dripped onto an uneaten custard cream on the parrot tray while Tony continued to drink his coffee, blissfully unaware of my predicament. I let out an ear splitting scream.

Tony wasn't given to leaping around. He always thought first – sometimes long and hard before saying or doing anything – so I was relieved as well as shocked at the speed with which he leapt up and grabbed Bertie around his body. My thumb was instantly released, and the parrot rubbed his head on Tony's sleeve. 'Brr brr.' Tony ignored Bertie and after dumping him back on his stand, gave my thumb his full attention. It was still bleeding, a bit slower now, but a good half of the nail was detached from its bed. Tony was horrified, in his quiet way. 'Oh dear, what has he done?'

'Nothing much; just tried to REMOVE MY THUMB NAIL.' I malevolently looked across at Bertie, who was head banging to Kylie Minogue's 'I should be so lucky …'

Bertie didn't like Anna, either, but she was quite happy about it as the feeling was mutual. He tolerated my eldest daughter Lisa, and allowed her to stroke him – sometimes, if he didn't want her attention, he walked away from her rather than bite her. But the love of his life was Tony. He had already learned the sound of the van and screeched at the top of his voice when he heard it, not stopping until Tony walked through the office door. They went to the kitchen together, where Bertie helped make the coffee by pulling off the lid of the cafetiere and getting the spoon out of the drawer for the sugar. He chose the biscuits each day; his favourites were chocolate bourbons. They were Tony's favourites too …

Trying to clean his stand required some very specialist equipment. Tony's gauntlets, which were standard issue to all RSPCA Inspectors and very useful when dealing with birds of prey, and a wooden broom handle. Sometimes Bertie grabbed one of the gauntlets with his beak and refused to let go. We used this to our advantage and dangled him across the office to the back of the desk chair, where he was happy to sit with pieces of fruit or some nuts to keep him occupied. Sometimes he climbed onto the broom handle for us. Whichever way he chose, it had to be done quickly. If he held onto the gauntlet, we transported him just above the floor so if he fell, he only fell an inch or so, but if he did fall, he was after us immediately.

'That bloody bird!' shouted Anna as she stomped across to the cat run I was cleaning. She was very red in the face. 'He wouldn't let go of the glove so I held it really low. He dropped to the floor, put his head down, spread his wings, and SQUAWKED as he charged at me. He lunged a few times and had me prancing around so much I must have looked like a bloody Morris dancer. He managed to get hold of my trouser leg with his beak and I was frantic. Then I remembered the fruit on the desk so I grabbed a grape and thankfully he preferred that to my leg. He's still on the floor but I've shut the door on him. Never thought cleaning up parrot shit could be so bloody dangerous.' She stomped back off again without waiting for a reply.

The broom handle was slightly better, it took him a few seconds to get to the end being held by the human, by which time we were able to turn it around, using the utmost care, and hopefully, deliver him to the back of the chair. If we didn't make it in time we had to put the broom handle down on the floor and leave the office. I'm ashamed to say that on more than one occasion I resorted to calling on Lisa, as Bertie was quite happy to climb onto her arm without trying to remove her nails. Lisa found it most amusing that her mother, the manager of the animal centre, couldn't deal with a parrot.

With the phone ringing many times throughout the day, Bertie discovered a new way to wreak havoc …

'Hello, RSPCA, Jane speaking, can I help you?'

'Yes, hello, I wonder if you could help me, I have this …'

'BRAH, BRAH, BRRRRAH, PREETY BOY, WHO'S A PREETY BOY …'

'RSPCA? Hello? Ah, there you are, some strange noises on …'

'BBBBRRRRRRRAAAAAAAAAAHHHHHHHH'

'Hello! Can you hear me? CAN YOU …'

Holding the phone to my ear with my left shoulder, I quickly peeled open a banana and shoved it at Bertie.

'Hello, it's Jane. I'm so sorry about that, we have a rather noisy parrot in the office. I can hear you perfectly now …'

We finished the rest of our conversation in peace, by which time Bertie would have thrown the banana skin on the floor and begun cracking open a walnut. I would watch as he lobbed the shell onto the floor, too. *The sooner we re-home you bird, the better,* was my only thought as I picked up his mess.

Marie was Anna's daughter, and she accompanied her mum to work as often as she could. She was fifteen, strong, and loved everyone, which seemed to be a family trait.

Bertie liked Marie. 'Say it, go on – Oh shit, oh shit, oh shit.' Marie spent her entire break trying to get Bertie to say it. 'Oh shit. Go on Bertie, you can do it.'

Anna was fed up with listening. 'Marie, will you bloody well pack it in? He's bad enough as it is the way he goes on every time the phone rings now. Imagine if he starts screeching out OH SHIT when one of us is trying to have a serious conversation!' She puffed at her menthol cigarette. 'Hasn't anyone offered him a home yet?' She looked at me.

'No. Every time I've had someone interested in him he's screeched at them and tried to bite them.'

'Hmm, that's what keeps happening with me too,' she replied. 'It was awful the other day. A man came in to look at cats and saw Bertie. He had a dog with him which kept leaping up towards the stand. I told him to be careful and he laughed and said it was okay, the dog wouldn't hurt the parrot. I said I wasn't worried about the dog hurting the parrot – I was worried about the parrot hurting the dog. Of course, despite being warned, the man got too close, the dog jumped up, Bertie lunged at it and got its ear. The dog yelped, the man shouted, Bertie let go and the dog's ear bled all over the place. What can you do if people don't listen?'

I was giggling at Anna's description of the event when the phone rang. We stopped and looked at each other.

'BRAAAHH …'

Marie had competition. 'Tony – Tony – Tony,' said Tony, in between munching on a chocolate bourbon. Bertie perched

47

on his chest and broke off bits of the biscuit until he got to the cream, his favourite bit.

'Tony – Tony … '

'For Christ's sake, will you stop saying TonyTonyTony to that damn parrot!' (It was my turn now.) 'I'm sick of hearing it, it's driving me nuts. Isn't being called preety boy all the time good enough for you?'

'Oh dear, I'm getting told off now, Bertie,' he said to the parrot, who had climbed down Tony to dip his beak into the coffee before helping himself to a piece of chocolate digestive. Muttering under my breath, I shook my head and left them to it.

Time passed and we all settled into a parrot-friendly pattern. We agreed that it was pointless for either Anna or myself to try and clean the stand (explaining to members of the public that we couldn't go into the office because there was a parrot loose on the floor was very embarrassing) so Lisa was voted chief parrot-stand cleaner, with Marie agreeing to do the deed at weekends as long as she was allowed to continue teaching Bertie to say 'Oh shit.' Anna agreed for the sake of peace.

I continued to give Bertie treats, but since he had tried to take my thumb nail off, I put the treats on the end of a fork, and it worked well. Anna took the fork thing a step further and pronged hazelnuts or bits of fruit ready for when the phone rang. Peace reigned and working life was good again, until Bertie's behaviour changed. He stopped shrieking when the phone rang, and became much less aggressive. He didn't even want to flap his wings and dance to Jon Bon Jovi songs while Marie played an imaginary guitar, and this had become one of his favourite pastimes.

'Tony, you will have to take him to the vets. He can't carry on like this; he's been quiet for about a week now. Today, he hasn't eaten, moved or shrieked – hasn't even had a poo yet, and you know how much of that he does.' Tony agreed, so I made an appointment for that afternoon.

'Hello. What's the matter with you then, eh?' Tony put his arm out to Bertie, who ignored it. I could see the worry in the frown on his face. 'He really isn't right, is he?' Tony continued.

'No.' I didn't want to talk about it because much as I'd hated the bird, he had character, oodles of it, and I'd already teared-up a few times when I'd looked at him. I surprised myself at how upset I was thinking he may have something seriously wrong with him. 'I've made you a small coffee, which you just have time to drink before you go, so come on, hurry up.' My abruptness towards Tony was to hide my real feelings.

Anna sat at the desk and said nothing. She was trying to fill in a food order form, but as I went back out to get our tea, I noticed it was still blank.

We tried to talk about the food order, but got no further than how many sacks of dog biscuit we needed before we lapsed into silence. I glanced sideways at Bertie, who was now sitting in his favourite place on Tony's chest, with his head hanging. Tears stung my eyes so I stood up and went to look out of the window.

'Bertie, what's wrong?' Tony brought us out of our reverie. The bird was now shifting from one leg to the other, and groaning. 'Oh Bertie,' said Tony quietly as he stroked the bird's head.

'Brrh.' Bertie lifted his tail slightly, lowered and pushed out his bottom, and dropped a small, white egg onto Tony's jumper. It rolled off and smashed onto the tiled floor. Bertie shook himself, and headed for the table. Astonished, and in silence, we watched as he slurped at the coffee, and helped himself to a digestive before going back onto Tony's chest for a good preen. Several seconds went by before anyone spoke.

'He's a she then,' said Anna.

'It would appear so,' said Tony.

'I can't believe I was so bloody worried about a … pregnant parrot,' I said.

We laughed, with relief and happiness, and I cancelled the vet visit.

The squawking coming from the office a couple of days later alerted me to Tony's arrival. Bertie was back on form and begrudgingly I had to admit that I was pleased.

Tony had brought in a young rabbit for re-homing, so we made our way to the 'summer house' which was a glorified shed situated on a grassy mound in the middle of the animal centre. There were large windows on both sides as well as in the doors and it was an ideal place for all the miscellaneous animals to stay until they were adopted.

'BRAH – BRRAH,' shouted Bertie. We continued across the grass, ignoring the screeching. 'BRRAAH – TONY.' We stopped, and looked at each other. Tony wasn't given to grinning any more than he was to leaping, but the biggest grin had spread across his face right then.

Just as quickly, the grin disappeared, and a serious look took its place. 'I have to have her,' he said. I instantly imagined the mayhem to come, and thought of my mum, and what she already had to put up with, but I knew how much Bertie meant to him. I put my arm through his and continued towards the summer house. 'I know.'

That night Bertie came indoors. We had no idea just how much our lives were about to change ...

CHAPTER 5

To Catch a Colony

With Bertie happily ensconced next to the diamond-leaded window in our living room, the office was back to normal, and I was glad to have peace again. Never more so than when the phone rang, and it was a serious issue that needed dealing with.

'The cats attacked your sister?' I couldn't believe the woman had just said that.

'Yes. She remembers falling over one of them and then it yowling at her. There's loads of them you see, she doesn't even know herself how many there are. It started off with just three, but over the years they've had lots of kittens. They're all wild, well, one of them sits on her lap but the others only let her stroke them when they're eating. Interbred, that's what they are – wouldn't be surprised if that's why they bit her. The lot of them are tabby you know, never did like any of them myself. She spends so much of her pension on food for them she doesn't have enough money to feed herself and now ends up in hospital. Anyway, she passed out, and when she woke up a big bit of her left calf had gone. She's in her eighties now, you know, and she's lucky she didn't break any bones. When she came round she somehow managed to drag herself to the phone and call me. I had to get a neighbour to take me over to her and he called for an ambulance. Neither of us had ever seen anything like it.'

The thought of cats doing this to an elderly lady who had been feeding them for years was abhorrent. 'Is your sister at home now?'

'No, she's in hospital still, fourth day today. They've put a bandage all the way up her leg but they say it will take months for it to heal, that's if it does heal. They should operate on it but they're worried about her heart. It'll be a last resort, but they will do it if the hole looks like it's going nasty. My dear, I want those cats out of there, now. The doctor won't let my sister home until they're all gone. He says all of them should be put to sleep and I have to say I agree with him.'

I bristled at the thought of destroying them all indiscriminately. 'Well, let's just wait and see before we make any decisions like that, shall we? Can I have your sister's address? I'll go and have a look, see if any of them are around.' I wrote down the details and told the woman I would go the following day.

I later found out the cats had originally come from an old brewery down the road, which had closed some years before. Once the place was deserted the woman had encouraged the cats to move in with her because she was alone and glad of their company. Having fed the cats for so many years, I wondered how she felt about them now she was in hospital with a hole in her leg. And I wondered how she would feel about them all being put to sleep. Maybe it would be her choice too, but somehow I didn't think so.

The unadopted road was full of potholes and difficult to navigate in my battered old Sherpa van, but I persevered and a few minutes later pulled up next to the static caravan that was the woman's home. Cats were everywhere. I tried to count them but they slunk around, moving away from me whenever I got too close, and because they were all tabby it was difficult to know for sure, but I thought there must have been at least eleven or twelve.

The caravan was unlocked, and although I didn't usually go into someone's home without them or someone else being present, the sister had told me to go inside. The cats were able to get in through the windows, and she wanted to make sure the whole lot of them were gone before her sister came home.

A small porch had been added on one side and housed a washing machine and a gardening table, under which was a multitude of different sized flower pots covered in dusty cobwebs. Along the window sills were tomatoes, all in different stages of ripening, and a dozen or so empty glass milk bottles. The floor was littered with baking trays and plates, all with the dried-up remnants of the cats' last meal.

As I opened the door to go inside, a cat limped out, hissing at me as it went. I gasped in horror; its back was twisted in a curve and looked grotesque. 'Oh my God,' I whispered. Shocked, I watched the cat until it disappeared under a bush.

All the curtains were closed and it took me a while to adjust to the dimness inside, but I couldn't mistake the shapes of yet more cats – on the bed, the book shelf, the top of the television. There were at least another eight in there, making about twenty altogether. *Oh boy, this is not going to be easy,* I thought. I closed the door and walked back to my van, feeling umpteen pairs of eyes watching me as I went. As I drove away, my thoughts went to the poor cat with the strange-looking back.

The traps we used to catch cats were about one foot square in cross section and two feet long and made of wire mesh. As soon as a cat stood on the metal plate at the far end, which was situated just in front of the food, the door was released and swung down, containing the cat.

I opened up the back doors of my van. 'We've got two traps, so with yours that makes five. Do you think the vets will have any we can borrow?' I asked Tony as he passed the traps to me.

'I doubt it, they don't really need them, do they? But no harm in asking. I'll go and give them a ring.'

I went to the kitchen and selected a variety of tinned cat food to use as bait.

'The vets don't have any traps but they can lend you some ordinary cat baskets if you need them.'

'OK thanks, I'll set these and will just have to see how it goes. They should be really hungry by now, so hopefully they'll go straight into them.'

As I drove through the gate Tony stopped me. 'Good luck.'

'Thanks. I'm feeling quite positive but I think I'm going to need some luck too.' I blew him a kiss and drove off.

With the traps set under various bushes in the garden, and lots of hungry cats watching, I decided to wait around for a while in the hope that something would happen. We had five cat units ready and waiting in the cattery, so all I had to do now was catch them. I sat in the van, lit a cigarette, and waited.

An hour later not a single cat had gone near those traps. *Right. They're obviously not stupid. They don't like strange smells or strange people.* I started the engine. *OK –* I looked at a pair of eyes in the bushes – *I'll leave you lot to it for a while, but I'll be back.* They watched me as I reversed. *You won't be able to resist the food for long …*

Empty. Untouched. All of them. Nothing but bluebottles buzzing around on the meat, which had baked in the heat of the sun and was covered in hundreds of fly eggs. I looked around me, and felt like I was in a scene from Alfred Hitchcock's 'The Birds', except with cats. Cats stared at me: from under bushes, on the fence, in an ancient, moss-covered apple tree, on the roofs of the caravan and porch. They didn't move; they just stared.

It was hot and dusty, but a chill went down my spine and I shivered as goose bumps appeared on my arms. My imagination ran away with me as I thought about the old lady, lying in hospital with a hole in her leg; a hole made by these cats. *Don't be stupid,* I chided myself as I stared back at them. *They are cats – just cats.* I forced myself to walk towards one of them and it backed away into a bush. *Yep, just cats.*

I collected the traps and tipped the already foul smelling food out into a carrier bag to take back and dispose of. I didn't think they would eat it now even if they were hungry, but I wasn't going to ruin my chances of catching them by leaving it there. Using a dustpan and brush, I reached into each trap and brushed out as much of the meat as I could, then replaced it with fresh chunks. I took a last look around, and sighed. *Now then, let's see what happens tonight, you stubborn little buggers. You must be starving, so get yourselves in there.* Feeling less than positive, I drove home.

Next day, Anna called as I was opening the gate to go back. 'Jane – before you go, Mrs Johnson is on the phone. She asked if you'd got the cats yet. I told her it's only been a couple of days and it would take time, and that you were just off there now, but she wants to speak to you.'

'What? I know she wants rid of them but blimey.'

I walked back to the office. 'Hello, Mrs Johnson. I'm off there now to see if any are in the traps. They are very scared of strangers and wouldn't go near them yesterday, so it's probably going to take a while.'

'My dear, I don't mean to pester you but those cats must go. I'm very disappointed that you haven't caught any yet. The doctor won't let my sister back there until they're all gone, as you know. You will try harder today, won't you.' It was a statement rather than a request.

My face burned with indignation. 'I really am doing my best, Mrs Johnson. As soon as I've trapped one I'll phone you.'

Replacing the phone, I looked at Anna. 'Wish the cats were as bloody keen as Mrs Johnson is. See you later.' Anna gave me an understanding smile as she closed the gate behind me.

Empty, again; and about twenty pairs of eyes watched me as for the second time I tipped out the meat. *'What is it with you lot? Why the hell aren't you going in the traps? You must be starving; you haven't been fed for days now …'* The thought of having to tell Mrs Johnson I still hadn't trapped any cats wasn't a very pleasant one. Disheartened, I sat down on one of the traps and looked around for inspiration.

They were fed in the porch every day, so I set a trap on the floor in there, and surrounded it with small amounts of food on the plates. Straight away I noticed some movement out of the corner of my eye so I went and stood on the far side of my van to watch.

Within just a few minutes, several of the cats slunk over to the food, grabbed a mouthful and ran off with it. *Success!* Well, it was a start anyway. Replenishing the food, I decided to leave them to get used to the trap being there, and left.

Dread filled me as I pulled up the next morning, but it changed to glee as I found not just one cat caught in the trap, but two. *Yes! Oh you little beauties.* I knelt down next to them. Both were very thin, but neither had runny eyes or snotty noses, and their coats looked OK. I took the full trap to my van and covered it in a sheet to help make the cats feel as safe as possible, then went back to set up the others in the porch – one on the garden table, and three on the floor.

I drove even more slowly down the bumpy road, conscious of the fear that the two cats must be feeling, having never been contained, or in a vehicle before. 'Come on, little ones, let's get you out of here.' I was glad that there were two cats; at least they were company for each other in their scary new life.

The trapped cats were very nervous as they went into their temporary home, and both slunk into a cardboard box at the back of the unit. Bless Anna, she'd taped up the box and cut a hole in the side for them to get in and out, which would hopefully make them feel safer. With fresh food and water just outside the box and a litter tray right next to it, there was nothing else I could do except leave them to settle in.

'Mrs Johnson? Hello, it's Jane from the RSPCA. I'm sure you'll be very pleased to know I've caught two cats, both in one trap!' My spirit soared as I imparted the information.

'Hello dear. Is that all? I'll phone the doctor but I'm not very happy about it and I know he won't be either.'

Deflated, I replaced the receiver. A postcard that had been pinned to a wall in my dad's workshop for many years came to mind: We do the impossible at once. Miracles take a little longer …

Over the following week it was with a huge amount of relief that I took eighteen cats back to the animal centre with me, which filled up the five units. By this time I had already realised that my original estimate of about twenty was out; I could still see more than ten pairs of eyes out there as I looked around, but with the units already so full, trapping had to be temporarily suspended.

'Hello, Mrs Johnson. No, I haven't caught them all yet. Yes, I know how long it's been but … Yes I am thinking about your sister. I've caught twenty so far but there are still at least ten more. Yes I am trying hard. I'm sorry the doctor thinks they should all be killed, Mrs Johnson, but fortunately for them he's the doctor and I'm the one doing the catching, and I have no intention of killing them all just because he says so. Yes, I do need to use the word killed, Mrs Johnson; that's what putting an animal to sleep means …'

While I had been busy catching them, Anna had been booking them in to the vets for check-ups and neutering, and some of them had already been done. They were all fit and healthy, and the vet estimated their ages as being between one and seven years, so we didn't anticipate any problems re-homing them, even though they were feral. There were many livery yards and private stable blocks in our area, and most were happy to have a couple of feral cats to keep the rats down, so Anna put a plea in the local paper, and the response was amazing. Pending the outcome of the home-checks, we had offers of homes for at least twenty-two cats, and not just from livery yards, so we were ecstatic.

The vet could only guess the ages of the cats by the condition of their teeth, but on this we paired them up as best we could, so that youngsters went together, and older ones did too. So far, so good, and with some of them going off to their new homes, I went to set the traps once again.

'Here we are then. You lot hungry?' Numerous pairs of eyes watched me. 'Duck flavour this time; come on.' I wafted the food around before putting it in the traps, trying to encourage them.

Another nine cats were caught during the week, one of them being the cat with the strange-looking back, which upon examination showed a deformity in its spine. The vet had our permission to euthanize any animal that he felt necessary, and this one he did. Afterwards he showed me the X-ray, and pointed out the twisted bones. He explained that the cat would have been in a lot of pain, and as it aged, the pain would increase because the tissue between the vertebrae was being squashed more as the spine continued to bend. Euthanasia was always a last resort; but for this little cat it was the only option.

Knowing the cat had been put to sleep was upsetting, but the pain it must have suffered was unimaginable so there had been no choice.

Every day for the next eight days I replenished the traps with fresh food, but although there were at least six more cats to be caught, the traps remained empty.

'Hello, Mrs Johnson. No, I haven't been avoiding you. Yes, I've still only caught twenty-nine. Yes, there are still about six left. No, I can't force them into the traps. Pardon? There's no need to be rude, Mrs Johnson, I can only do what I can do. You're what?' The phone went dead.

'ANNA,' I shouted outside the office door.

'YO,' she called back, from the area of the dog exercise runs. I made my way up the slight hill towards her, trying to light a cigarette as I went.

'Mrs Johnson is threatening to call in pest control to get the rest of the cats. And she's just put the phone down on me.' I lit another match which was promptly blown out by the wind.

'She said that to me a couple of days ago,' Anna informed me, belatedly. 'I told her it wasn't necessary, and you'd catch them all, but she'd have to be patient. Don't worry, I don't think they do cats anyway, do they?' Anna, having watched me light several more matches but not my cigarette, gave me her lighter.

'Thanks. I can't believe that woman. How rude of her to put the phone down on me! I've done everything I can; what does she want, for God's sake …?' I inhaled deeply.

'Your blood? Honestly, Jane, don't worry about it. She won't get pest control in, I'm sure of it.'

The next morning I couldn't park in my usual place – the pest control van was in the way.

'Morning,' I called out to the man who was poking around under a bush.

'Morning. I hear you're having problems catching some cats. I've been asked to come and do the job for you.' He leant against the side of the static as he gave me a lop-sided, know-it-all grin.

My hackles were well and truly up. 'Great, thanks for the offer, but having spent ages catching the other twenty-nine, I'd quite like to finish the job myself – if that's okay with you?'

The man stopped grinning. 'You've already caught twenty-nine?'

'Yes – I've already caught twenty-nine.'

'Oh, well no-one told me that bit. In that case I reckon I'd feel the same as you do, love, don't worry – I know when I'm not wanted.' He smiled, a nice smile, and winked at me as he went out of the gate. 'I saw the traps in the porch; nothing I could do that you aren't doing anyway, so you carry on.'

I smiled back at him and regretted my attitude. 'Thanks, I appreciate that.'

'Like I said, love, I'd feel the same. Have fun. See you.' He waved as he went.

Phew, what a relief. He was such a nice bloke. Right then – where were we? I looked at the traps and my heart sank. *Oh sod it – empty again …*

Realising it was pointless to re-set them, I took the traps back to my van and lined up four plates full of food just inside the static, leaving the door wide open. *Please …*

Feral cats dominated my thoughts that evening.

Next day, the sun beat down and even though it was only nine in the morning, it was uncomfortably hot. Carrying a grasper in one hand and a cat basket in the other, I walked towards the porch. No pairs of eyes stared at me from under bushes or in trees. All of the food had been eaten. Quietly, I went into the caravan and closed the door. Six cats were dotted around the living room, watching as I closed the door. Relief flooded through me; I had them all now, and just had to catch them.

There were no doors inside the static, not even to the bathroom, which had a heavy red velvet curtain instead, so I would have to catch the cats in the porch, it was my only choice.

'RIGHT. OUT. COME ON ALL OF YOU, OUT.' Waving my arms about at the same time as shouting, I walked around the edge of the living room and watched smugly as the six cats disappeared into the porch. With the static door closed they were now contained in as small an area as I could get them. So this was it – at last.

There was a small gap between the back of the washing machine and the wall, and all of them had somehow managed to wedge themselves on top of each other into the space. I opened the lid of the cat basket and leaning over the top of the washing machine, lowered the grasper over the head of the nearest one to me. The cat froze and allowed me to tighten the noose around its neck and lift it into the basket without a struggle. *Oh thank God. One down – five to go …*

I expected the cat to try and escape from the basket as I opened it to put in the second cat, but it squashed itself down against the wire floor instead. *Two down – four to go ...*

The last four didn't move from behind the washing machine when I opened the porch door to go and get two more baskets, either.

This is too easy. Five down – one to go ...

As I lowered the grasper over the last cat's head, I noticed its left ear was mangled and hairless, and wondered if this was another deformity. The cat moved, and with an agility I never imagined possible, leapt backwards onto the window sill, scattering tomatoes and milk bottles in its wake. Glass smashed in all directions and over-ripe tomatoes burst as they hit the floor. The cat stopped and stood on its hind legs, meowing pitifully and pawing at the door before flying back along the sill, and dropping down behind the washing machine once more.

More attempts with the grasper failed, so I hauled the heavy machine further away from the wall and got into the gap, taking an old donkey jacket from a nail on the wall as I went. The cat didn't move as I laid the jacket over its body and very slowly tucked it underneath, encasing the cat completely.

Just as I got the lid of the basket open, a frenzied attack began on the donkey jacket and my fingers. Teeth and claws worked in harmony as I fumbled, trying desperately not to lose the cat as I disentangled it from the jacket until finally I closed the lid. Trembling, I looked at my hands. Both were peppered with bites and scratches, far too many to count, and covered in blood. I suddenly realised that I was in serious pain.

Four days later I laughed with Anna as I tried, unsuccessfully, to hang a water bottle on the side of a rabbit hutch, with hands throbbing, swollen and oozing pus. As I picked the bottle up from the floor for the third time, Tony stopped me. 'I know you think it's funny, but you're going to have to see someone whether you like it or not. I'm taking you up to Accident and Emergency: now. No argument. Look at your arm …'

Tony drew his finger along the inside of my arm, from the vein in my wrist, almost to my elbow, following a red line just under the skin.

'What is it?' I had stopped laughing.

'You've got an infection, and it needs treating. Come on,' Tony replied.

'Oh for goodness' sake, it's nothing. I'm not going to waste their time, I'm fine.'

'You may feel fine now but that red line is going towards your heart. I know because I had the same problem a few years ago and ended up having the back of my hand opened up under general anaesthetic. I had to have antibiotics by drip … Come ON.'

Sufficiently worried, I told Anna I wouldn't be long and followed Tony to his van.

'Hello, you're still alive then,' said Anna, when, several hours later, we got back to the centre. 'Ha-ha! You look just like a mummy!'

'Am I alive? I feel worse now than I did before. They've prodded and poked and flushed out all the puncture wounds with antiseptic and shoved cream all over them. Then they injected me with antibiotics.' I flopped onto the comfy armchair with Anna's dogs, 'Apparently I've got Cat Scratch Fever and they've given me a pile of pills to take.' I held my hands up and studied the vast amount of bandaging that covered them, 'And how on earth am I going to take them – or hold a cup of tea?'

Over the next two weeks Mrs Johnson's sister was allowed home, my hands began to heal, and the cat that had mauled me gave birth to four kittens, all tabbies, of course.

'Hello, RSPCA, Jane speaking.'

'I'd like to talk to you, if you wouldn't mind. I need to know what you've done with them.'

'Erm … done with what?'

'I know my sister and the doctor wanted them all put to sleep … Did you … put them to sleep? I don't know why I'm asking really, I think I know what the answer is.'

'No,' I replied gently to the lady, who sounded so near to tears. 'We didn't put them all to sleep.'

'You didn't?' Her voice cracked as she whispered. 'Thank you, they meant everything to me. I miss them …'

Before putting the receiver down, I realised I didn't even know her name.

I visited Vera twice over the next couple of months, and found that she blamed herself, not the cats. If she hadn't fallen on top of one, it wouldn't have happened. She cried with relief when she knew that they had been re-homed, and with sadness when I told her about the one that had to be put to sleep. She especially missed the one with the funny ear, as that was the one that happily spent hours sitting on her lap as she knitted. The place was empty now …

'Hi, Vera, it's Jane from the RSPCA,' I called as I knocked on the porch door.

'Hello dear, come in, come in. How are you? Would you like a cup of tea?'

'Love one, please. Oh, and I've got something for you.'

'Have you, what's that dear?' Vera replied.

I lifted the cat basket from behind the hedge, and held up the cat with the mangled ear. 'I thought you could do with some company.'

She put both hands up to her face and for several seconds didn't move. Her tears fell silently as she then embraced the basket.

'Feo,' she said quietly, as she opened the basket and lifted the cat out. It immediately wrapped itself around her legs, purring as it did.

Vera held out her hands to me. 'Thank you. Thank you.'

Through a blur of my own tears I took her hands and mumbled that it was the least I could do.

I gave her a hug. 'Don't worry about the tea – you've got some catching up to do.'

CHAPTER 6

Like Chalk and Cheese

Tom looked distinguished. His spotless grey uniform, whose buttons were like polished silver, was made for his tall, slim frame. The trousers bore a perfect crease down the front of each leg. He loved his job and wore his uniform with pride. He was a real gentleman.

Tom was the dog warden, employed by the local council, and as the animal centre had a contract to board stray dogs as a way of raising funds, we saw quite a lot of him.

'Good morning, Tom.'

'Good morning, Jane, and what a lovely morning too.'

'Yes it is. Are you bringing in or collecting today?'

'I have been requested by the police to collect two dogs from a property. The owner has been arrested and is likely to be detained indefinitely. I believe a large quantity of an illegal substance has been found in his possession. As the dogs are not stray, the council won't be liable to pay for their board-ing. However, the police assure me that they will meet any charges incurred during the dogs' stay.'

'Hmm … I'm happy to take them in but I think it would be better if they could be signed over to us by the owner,

Tom, if that's possible. We've only recently re-homed a dog that was brought in by the police seven months ago. It's not about the money; it's more about the fact that we can't re-home an animal unless it's been signed over to us. The owner was supposed to pay the boarding fee and have the dog back, but he disappeared and we got left with the poor dog and no money.'

'I fully understand, Jane, and will make sure that a signature is obtained prior to the removal of the dogs.'

'Thanks, Tom, I'd appreciate that; it avoids any possible problems with the owner coming back and trying to claim them after they've been adopted by someone else. I'll get a kennel ready for them – see you later.' Tom strode off down the driveway.

We had two isolation kennels which we used only for emergencies, but as they were well away from all the noise and bustle of the rest of the centre, I decided that the two dogs should go into the farthest one. I put fresh water, clean bedding, several toys and a couple of chew knots in it ready for their arrival.

On his return, I noticed that Tom had a piece of blood-covered tissue wrapped around the hand he used to open the back door of his van. I raised my eyebrows but said nothing.

'Here we are then,' he said, as I peered into the gloom to see a friendly tail wagging on the dog tied to the left side of the van, while the one on the right showed me a lovely set of teeth. Its lower jaw dripped a mixture of saliva and blood onto the rubber floor of the van and the dog trembled uncontrollably as I looked at it.

'I must warn you, Jane, the tan and white is not at all friendly.' Tom held up his hand as if to prove what he was saying. 'Although she is quite small, I had to put a grasper on her in the end, there really was no alternative. I think she has bitten her tongue in her efforts to escape from it.'

He undid the tissue as he spoke and exposed two deep and very nasty puncture wounds where the canine teeth had sunk into both the palm, and the back of his hand. After studying it for just a moment, he calmly wrapped the tissue back around his hand and continued.

'They are mongrels – sisters; aged approximately two-and-a-half years, and I believe the black and white one is pregnant. I have a letter here that the police made the owner write, which signs both of the dogs over to the RSPCA for re-homing. The black and white dog is called Tina, the tan and white, Trix.'

'Tom – your hand …'

'I'm more concerned with the dogs at this moment. There was no food at the property, and the owner hadn't been there for several days, so we have no idea when they were last fed. If you'd like to take Tina, I will attempt to follow with Trix.'

'No, Tom. You'll stay here while I take Tina, and then I'll come back for Trix – no argument.' I untied the lead, calling Tina as I did so, and she obediently hopped out of the van. She waddled happily along behind me and sat down in the kennel as soon as I closed the door on her.

Trix was another matter. I spoke to the dog in a soft voice as I untied the handle of the grasper, and gently pulled. She made a high-pitched noise that sounded like a cross between a growl and a scream, and attacked the handle with a ferocity I didn't expect from a dog the size of a King Charles spaniel.

'Hey ... calm down, little one.' I tried to placate her, but she writhed around on her back and continued to attack the handle, all the while screaming and gurgling as if I was killing her. I loosened the noose around her neck, just slightly, and hoped she would feel better once she was out of the van, but blood spattered everywhere as she leapt into the air, and with front paws wrapped around the handle, she repeatedly bit at the metal in an attempt to free herself. My heart was pumping like mad; I had to tighten the noose again for fear that she would escape and die somewhere, alone and afraid. What the hell do you do with a dog like this? Shocked, I looked at Tom and shouted, 'Jesus, Tom, how did you get her into the van?'

'Like this,' said Tom.

Even more shocked, I watched this most gentle of men grab the grasper from me, and half lifting, half dragging, haul Trix up to the kennel where Tina stood wagging her tail. I ran ahead and opened the door ready. Like lightning, Tom dropped the dog into the bed and pulled the release wire on the grasper. I slammed the door shut on the dogs.

Tom leaned his back against the wall and blood dripped off the saturated tissue round his hand as his chest heaved in and out.

'Tom ... oh shit, Tom ... I've never seen anything like it before ...'

I looked at the dog who was now cowering at the back of the kennel, then at Tina, who stood at the bars, still wagging her tail, then back to Tom, who hadn't moved for what seemed like for ever, and my legs suddenly turned to jelly.

'I've put extra sugar in your tea, Tom.' I think I was the one needing the extra sugar, and I was dying for a cigarette, but refrained, as Tom didn't smoke.

'Thank you, I appreciate your kindness,' Tom replied. 'I'm very upset about this. It's really rather sad.'

'Tom – I'm so sorry. I've used a grasper a few times now, but none of the dogs behaved like that. It completely took me by surprise.'

'My dear, you have no need to apologise – I mean I'm upset about the poor little dog. She is only aggressive because she's petrified. I don't believe she would generally behave in such a way. It's most unpleasant when one has to man-handle an animal in such a fashion, but unavoidable on occasions. I would much rather be firm and quick, it's less traumatic for the animal. You mustn't feel bad that you were unsure what to do. You will gain confidence with experience, it's the only way.'

I looked at Tom with renewed respect.

'Trix … Trixtrix. Come on then …' Even my softest, sing-song voice wasn't going to persuade her that I wasn't going to hurt her. Every day for the next week I spent hours trying to get closer to her, but she hid behind the bed at the back of the kennel and growled if I tried to get too close.

I looked at my watch. I'd been sitting for a good hour on a blanket on the floor right next to the dog bed, reading aloud so that she got used to me, but it was almost midnight and enough was enough. As I stretched, the usual growl erupted.

'Oh Trix – you can't stay there forever ...' I pulled the bed away from the wall, talking quietly, and as I reached down towards her, she lunged at my hand, just missing me by a fraction of an inch, before crouching back against the wall. The snapping of the teeth as they met resounded in the small space of the kennel, and as I looked at this poor, terrified little dog, I wondered what on earth we were going to do with her.

Tom had visited Trix at every opportunity, even bringing his wife along one evening when they were on their way out for a drive. Despite the delicious-smelling casseroled liver, the crispy chicken skin, or the pork crackling that both he and his wife offered, Trix stayed behind the bed.

'Well. What else can we do?' he said to me when the dogs had been in the kennel for nearly two weeks. 'One would have thought that seeing Tina so happy to accept food from us, Trix would have realised by now that we are no threat to her.'

'I know. Nothing works – and Tina looks like she's due to give birth at any time now. Anna is very concerned about when the pups are born; we obviously don't know what Trix will be like towards them, and she wants to move Tina into another kennel, but I'm worried that it will make things worse.' I paused before continuing, 'I've asked the vet for his opinion about what to do with her, Tom. He thinks it's going to be difficult to re-home her because she has an unsound temperament.' My voice cracked and went a few notes higher. 'In his opinion I should have her humanely destroyed ...'

Tom's head dropped and seconds passed. 'Yes. Yes, I can understand why he feels that's the right thing to do. Jane – I feel for her. I realise that you have to make the right decision, for her sake, as well as for the RSPCA, but … time, perhaps she needs just a little more time. I know you will make the right decision.' With his head still hanging, he walked away from the kennel.

At that moment I didn't know who I felt most sorry for – Trix, Tom, or me.

The following morning Anna rushed past with a bowl of milk, shouting as she went, 'She keeps whining Jane, I think she's started. She keeps pawing at the door so I'm just going to give her a drop of warm milk. I don't think she wants to be in the kennel so I might let her have a little wander around for a while.'

'OK,' I called out to her back.

Anna fussed around Tina all morning, even offering her ham sandwiches, which the dog ate willingly. And if Tina didn't want one of the many bowls of warm milk she was offered, Anna made her a bowl of tea instead. 'She must keep her strength up, she's got some hard work ahead of her and we don't want her getting dehydrated,' was Anna's reasoning.

Tina did plenty of wandering, closely followed by Anna, and each time ended up on the comfy old armchair in the corner of the office, much to the annoyance of Anna's dogs who regarded it as theirs. They looked most indignant when Anna offered them a blanket on the floor.

'Oh – she's doing little strains. I'm going to have to get her back into the kennel,' called Anna across the office. It was full of people, a busy Saturday morning, with members of the public looking around, buying food and toys, and adopting animals from us; the last thing we needed was a dog going into labour on the armchair in the office. But Tina wasn't at all bothered about the people. Refusing to move, she wagged her tail and seemed to be lapping up all the attention she was receiving as Anna explained to the amused onlookers that the dog was about to give birth.

With Anna on her knees in front of the armchair and taking on the role of midwife, I was grateful Marie was working that day, and called her for the umpteenth time. 'Could you get me a sack of biscuit from the shed please? And put it into the boot of Mrs Crane's car? Thanks. And then could you get Flopsy and Mopsy rabbits please? They are going home today. The new owners need a carrying box to put them in too, could you make one up for me please? Thanks. Oh, and could you ...'

At one o'clock I thankfully put the closed sign on the gate, and went into the kitchen to make tea for the three of us, and for Tina, and as I walked back into the office Tina produced her first pup.

'It's a boy!' exclaimed Anna, as she held up the black and white pup for us to see. Fascinated, I watched the new mum lick her puppy from top to bottom and back again as it squirmed its way towards her teats, and marvelled at the natural instinct in them both.

During lunch break, Tina drank a further two bowls of tea, ate a fried egg sandwich, and gave birth to three more black and white pups, all girls. 'She still looks huge, like she's got loads more pups in there. Or is it all the tea and sandwiches?' I asked Anna, who hadn't moved the entire time, except to drink her tea, and sit on the chair that Marie had got for her.

'I think she's got more in there,' Anna replied. 'Ooh look, she's straining. Definitely more to come.'

I put the open sign on the gate and a new crowd of people entered the office. Enthralled, they stayed to watch Tina give birth to pup number five. I had already taken the names of those who wanted to adopt the previous four, so was waiting for the first person to ask for this one, when I noticed a little girl, aged about seven, crying as she watched.

'Are you OK?' I asked her.

'Yes, thank you.' The tears continued to fall down her cheeks.

'Where's your family?'

'They're looking at the dogs. Our dog has gone to heaven.'

Everyone else appeared to be listening, and a big, but quiet 'Ahh' erupted.

'Oh.' I didn't quite know what to say. 'That's very sad.'

'Sarah? Sarah?'

The little girl looked towards the door. 'I'm here, Mummy.'

A woman squeezed her way to the armchair and took the little girl's hand. 'Here you are! Don't you want to choose a new dog darling? You've been crying – what's wrong? Oh my …' The mother caught sight of Tina and her pups.

'She looks like Tina, Mummy. I wish we still had Tina. Can we have that one, Mummy – please?' The little girl pointed towards the armchair.

I smiled. Puppy number five now had a home. I went to the desk and got pen and paper to take down their details.

'You're right, Sarah, she looks very much like Tina did.'

I smiled at the little girl. 'So – your dog was called Tina, and the Mummy dog is called Tina too. What are you going to call your new puppy?' I had no doubt that the home-check would be fine, and so was confident that the little girl would have her pup.

The little girl stared at me, wide-eyed and open-mouthed. 'Her name is Tina too?'

'Yes,' I laughed, 'her name is Tina too!'

With a whoop of joy, Sarah put her arms around Tina's neck and hugged her. 'Tina, you are going to come and live with me, and we will play together and you can sleep in my bed sometimes, just like my other Tina did.'

Astonished, I looked at the mother. 'I thought she meant one of the pups.'

'No, she means Tina. It's such a coincidence; this Tina is an identical version of our Tina, but younger. Ever since our Tina died we've been wanting to come and look at the dogs but Sarah never wanted to – until today. Do you believe in fate?'

As I took the details from Sarah's mother, we discussed fate, and I told her yes – I did believe that some things were meant to be.

By four o'clock Tina had given birth to eight puppies, and all of them were already being held for their prospective new owners, although the one I was most pleased about was Tina, who I knew was going to love her new home. But my happiness for Tina was short-lived as I thought about Trix. *Oh God; Trix. Poor, poor Trix ...*

We decided to let Tina stay in the office with her pups, but Anna moved them into a plastic dog bed for the sake of safety, and for the sake of Anna's own dogs, who had not been amused at having to spend the entire day on a blanket on the floor. They had tried several times to jump onto the chair with Tina and were most put out when Anna shoved them off.

As Anna coaxed Tina out of her bed for a last wander, Marie took my five- and six-year-old daughters, Shanie and Kelley, off with her to hose out the dog runs. This was something they loved doing, especially getting the water out with the big, rubber scrapers. I was crouched down, having just locked the day's takings into the safe which was bolted to the floor behind the desk, when something landed on my lap and knocked me backwards. The wall stopped me from going over, and I looked with surprise at the dog now sitting on me, with its head buried under my arm, and I burst out laughing. My laughter turned to tears, as I lifted Trix's head up and she licked my cheek, and I stroked her for the very first time.

'MUM ... MUM! SHE'S GONE ...' Marie was shrieking at Anna. 'I don't know how she got out, but she did.'

'OH BUGGER!' shouted Anna, back at her. 'Which way did she go?'

'This way,' I said, standing in the doorway, with Trix in my arms.

They both stopped – and time went into slow motion as they both came over and made a fuss of Trix, who gently wagged her tail at them.

'Oh, there you are, you naughty dog, I've been looking for you,' said Shanie, my five-year-old.

'You've been looking for her?' I asked.

'Yes. I think she missed Tina, Mummy, so I let her out, but then she ran too fast and I lost her.'

I could cheerfully have killed my child at that moment, and assured myself that stern words would be had with her at bed time that evening.

'Good morning, Tom. How are you today?'

'Good morning, Jane. I'm well thank you. I see you have your shadow with you.'

My shadow growled from behind my legs in response to Tom's voice. I looked at Trix, and told her to shush. 'Sorry, Tom. She's great with everyone now, except you. She's so loving, I still find it hard to believe she's the same dog as was on the other end of the grasper that day.'

'It's a pleasure to have her growling at me, Jane, even after four months! At least she is alive and happy, which is all I would have asked for her. Time Jane, as I said; time, was what she needed. Nothing more.' We walked along, amiably.

It wasn't just time that she had needed; it was also the innocence of a trusting child …

CHAPTER 7

Ewe Dare!

As I sailed backwards, very ungracefully, through the air, I thought for the umpteenth time that something needed to be done about Lucy. And as my back crashed against the recently repaired post and rail fence, I decided that something had to be done quite soon.

While the ducks and chickens nipped in and out between the obese sheep's legs, pecking up the bits of corn and maize that she was flinging about in her efforts to shovel in as much food as she could, as quickly as possible, I sat on the ground and got my breath back.

'JA-ANE,' I heard Anna shout. 'There's a call for you … WHERE ARE YOOOO?'

Still winded, I croaked back, 'Ahem. I'm … here Anna,' and crawled into her view.

'Oh my God! Are you okay? Don't tell me – Lucy?'

'Yes. Lucy.' I gasped as I spoke. 'It was quite spectacular – an excellent sideways toss of the head; one of the more painful ones.' Anna helped me to my feet, but I remained bent over as the pain in my rib cage increased.

'That sheep is such a cow!' Anna retorted in anger, as she attempted to brush the dirt off my bottom without actually touching it. 'She's so fat and lazy she only moves when she wants to eat or shit – in fact, she does that where she's lying more often than not. And she's such a bloody pig …'

I sniggered. 'She'd make an excellent bull too – tossing me into the fence like that. Good job she hasn't got horns, I'd have been done for.'

'Yes,' said Anna, 'she can be a right stroppy mare when she wants.'

Giggling, Anna hooked her arm around me and helped me to the office to answer the phone.

Stiff and bruised the following morning, I rang our vet to ask for advice about Lucy.

Although it was a small animal practice which didn't normally deal with farm animals, the vet agreed to see Lucy as long as I took her to the surgery. I was surprised that he didn't want to visit her at the centre, but arranged an appointment for her to go there.

Lucy had already lived at the animal centre for several years when we arrived, and as far as we knew, she had never met another sheep in her life. She wore a leather dog collar, and, very occasionally, she allowed people to take her for a walk down the lane.

On the morning of the appointment, I stood outside the paddock while she ploughed her way through breakfast, and attached the lead to her collar as she ate. Tony came and put his arm around my waist as I watched her.

'Oh no; pain – I'm in lots of pain.' I grimaced as I removed his arm carefully.

'Sorry. I've put the ramp on the back of your van. I just hope it's going to be strong enough to take her weight.'

'I'm sure it will. I don't know what I'd do without you.' I smiled. He'd made the ramp specially, to make it easier to get her up into the back of my van.

'Come on then Lucy, your carriage awaits you.' I took the bowl of food from her and opened the gate. She snuffled around on the floor, picking up the smallest bits of food, but wouldn't move. Tony took the lead and pulled, but she was having none of it.

'How about this then?' I held the bowl in front of her, and we were off. She trotted happily along, grabbing a mouthful of food every few steps. Bending sideways with a bowl whilst half running did nothing for the pain in my rib cage, but we got to the ramp, and she followed the bowl up right into the back of the van.

'Wow! I never dreamed she'd go in just like that!' I beamed at Tony. 'I'd better get some more food then.' I gave him a hug. 'Brilliant ramp, love.'

'Don't forget; take enough food to be able to get her in and out at the other end. Now, are you sure you don't want me to come with you?'

'No, honestly, I'll be fine. I do ache, but it's better to keep moving, and I have control over her as long as the bowl is in front of her. Anyway, if I have any problems, I'm sure the vet can help me.' I stood on tip-toe and kissed him. 'Thanks again. Love you. See you later.'

I looked round at Lucy, who was totally unperturbed by the movement or sound of the van, and drove out of the gate.

The veterinary practice was in a converted house, on quite a large council estate, and at the end of a cul-de-sac. As I untied the lead in the back of the van, an elderly couple stopped to watch, and enjoyed the spectacle of a very fat sheep following a food bowl down a ramp. 'Good grief,' said the husband, 'her back's so wide and flat you could use her as a table!' They laughed together as they went on their way.

Okay, so far, so good. Just got to get inside and we'll be safe. I opened the waiting room door. *Oh shit. How the hell can I get her in …?* A woman sat right next to the door, with a rabbit on her lap, and I was worried that Lucy might bash it with her head as she walked through. *Don't panic – don't … panic.*

'Erm … excuse me. I'm sorry to be a pain, but I wondered if you would mind moving, just for a moment, just while I get my sheep through the door …' The woman smiled and moved to another chair, and I relaxed a bit.

'Come on Lucy, get in.' I shoved the bowl in front of her and she duly followed. The woman with the rabbit got up again and, still smiling, moved into the farthest corner, next to another woman with a Yorkshire Terrier, which sat quaking on her lap. That gave me more room to manoeuvre Lucy, and after a minute or so, we were settled, and Lucy stood looking around her with interest.

But not for long. Suddenly, she yanked me across the room, stood in front of the rabbit, and pushing her nose right into its fur, sniffed it all over. The rabbit froze, and the smile on its owner's face seemed to as well. I mumbled my most profuse apologies and grabbed the bowl of food I'd hidden under the chair. Lucy obediently followed the bowl back to the seat. I had already broken out into a sweat; now I started to pray.

I thought my prayers had been answered when the door to the consulting room opened and the veterinary nurse called the owner of the rabbit. But as the rabbit went in, a Border Collie came out, and all hell broke loose.

The Collie flew at Lucy, pulling its lead out of its elderly owner's hand. Then it crouched, close to the floor and, growling loudly, it circled Lucy, until it finally lunged and nipped her on the back of her leg. Lucy let out an indignant bleat before turning full circle and facing the dog. The dog lunged at her face, but Lucy was quick; she did a sideways toss of the head, and got the dog under its chin. The dog's head snapped backwards.

Oh my God! What have you done, Lucy? ... I didn't want to look for fear that the dog's neck had been broken.

I knew it hadn't when the furious dog leapt at her, but this time Lucy got her head under its body and tossed it high up into the air. The dog crash-landed onto a coffee table, scattering magazines everywhere, before it slid onto the floor. Not to be outdone, the dog shook itself and made for Lucy's stomach, but Lucy was already turning and bashed the dog again, sending it sideways, bowling wooden chairs over like they were skittles as it crashed into them.

The owner of the rabbit shut herself in the toilet, and the nurse pulled the elderly owner out of the way of the furore and took him behind the counter, where they watched, open-mouthed, in silence. I tried to grab the dog's lead and offer the bowl to Lucy but got confused and grabbed Lucy's lead and offered the bowl to the dog. They both ignored me as they squared up to each other once more, with Lucy, head down, stamping her front foot, circling the dog, just as it circled her.

Just as the dog lunged at Lucy again, I saw a familiar, size eleven boot stomp down onto the dog lead, and my heart leapt as I looked up and saw Tony. The relief was incredible, but short-lived, as Lucy took full advantage of the situation, and butted the Border Collie up the backside.

Tony calmly picked the dog up and took it behind the counter, then came back to me and Lucy. 'Have you seen the vet yet?' he asked, as if nothing had happened.

'No … we … not yet,' I answered.

'Right. I'll wait with you then.'

'Okay.' I was quietly bursting with emotion – relief, unshed tears; but mainly love.

The vet came out and asked why his nurse hadn't taken in the next client. The nurse called the rabbit's owner out of the toilet and into the consulting room, the Border Collie was shown out of the back door and I suddenly realised that the woman with the Yorkshire Terrier was still sitting in her chair and the dog was still sitting on her lap, quaking.

Lucy was duly seen, and I was advised that what she really needed was to live with other sheep. I agreed, and as the vet knew someone with a small flock of pet sheep, he'd ask if they would take her on.

It all happened very quickly. Within days Lucy was en-route to her new home – a six acre field, complete with its own shelter, lots of grass, and twelve normal-looking, sheep.

I met the owners, and they were very happy to help, although quite shocked at just how fat Lucy was, even though they had been warned.

I offered Lucy the bowl of food for the last time, just to get her out of the van, and couldn't help the tears. Then, as I enticed her into the field, she stopped and looked around her, and for the first time, she trembled. Uncertain that I was making the right decision now, I started to pull her back to the gate.

The lady noticed my tears, and probably my doubts. 'Please – don't worry about her, she'll be fine. It may take her a couple of days to get used to them, but she will get used to them, honestly. You know where she is; and you're welcome to visit her at any time. You have our number if you want to call us too. And – my name is Margaret.'

I thanked her, but felt that I was doing the wrong thing. Lucy didn't want to stay there, and she was the one pulling me towards the gate now.

'Look, I really think I'll just take her back home. Thanks though, for everything. She doesn't want to stay, and I don't want to force her. I know it's all for her benefit, but if she's scared, then she won't be happy.'

'What about leaving her here for the night? If you really think she should go with you tomorrow, then take her, but give her a chance; let her make her own mind up once she's been here for a while.' It was the first time the man had spoken, except to say hello, but what he said made sense, so I reluctantly agreed.

'I'm so sorry,' I said, tears streaming down my cheeks as I removed the lead from her collar. 'I feel like I'm abandoning her.'

'Don't apologise, we understand. Come back tomorrow and see her; make your mind up then,' the man replied.

'We'll go now, leave you to say goodbye to Lucy on your own. Come on, Malcolm.' Margaret touched her husband's arm, and together they left.

Lucy hadn't moved from the gate, but the inquisitive sheep were now surrounding her, although keeping their distance. They bleated, one after the other, but Lucy didn't respond.

'Oh Lucy.' I stroked her head. 'Am I doing the right thing? I wish I knew.'

Time passed, and the sheep lost interest and moved off in a group, munching as they went. Lucy sniffed at the grass, and took a bite. I watched as she slowly moved further away from the gate, and was soon far enough away from me that I felt it was okay to go. It was the hardest thing in the world to drive off and leave her there.

Early the next morning I visited the field; Lucy was way across the other side, and didn't even see me. She wasn't with the flock, but she wasn't too far away from them all either. Now – I knew I had to leave her there; let her realise that she was a sheep.

I didn't want to keep visiting her, stupidly believing that if she saw me, she might want to come back with me, so I went once more to remove her collar, but didn't go again until Malcolm phoned and asked me to.

'Hello, Jane. I wondered if you'd like to visit Lucy. I know you phone every couple of weeks, but I thought rather than us just telling you she's fine, and she's lost lots of weight, you might like to come and see her now. I think you will be pleased, as well as surprised. How about it?'

'You know, I think I will. I can see now I was being stupid, so it's time I went and saw her. Thank you so much,

Malcolm – I do appreciate everything you've done for both of us.'

The next day was my day off, so on the way to taking my dogs out for their morning walk I did a detour to Lucy's field.

Standing at the gate, I smiled as I watched a lamb gambolling around, jumping on and off its mother's back, while another lamb snuggled next to her, with its head lying across one of her front legs. The mother licked its head in little, short licks. I scanned the field but couldn't see Lucy, so went in to look around more closely. There was another sheep with two lambs, both running along the side of the hedge and back again, sometimes bumping into each other and falling over. I stopped and watched them for a while, enjoying their exuberance, before resuming my search.

All the way around the field, I craned my neck and squinted in the sun as I searched for Lucy. Then as I made my way back down the field, I heard her bleat and turned.

A slender sheep walked towards me and leaned her body against me, waiting for me to stroke her head. It was Lucy; and she remembered me.

The lambs played around us while Lucy and I reacquainted ourselves.

I cried as I stroked her head, because I could see she was so happy and contented; I cried because she had two beautiful lambs that she clearly loved; but mostly I cried because after not seeing me for over six months, she remembered me.

As I pulled out of the lay-by I looked in my rear view mirror, and the three of them were framed in it for a second or two. They were all lying down, with the lambs in front, and Lucy resting her head across both their backs, eyes closed.

It was a moment I would treasure for the rest of my life. Lucy had found herself. She was a real sheep now.

CHAPTER 8

Samson

I looked down the lane and couldn't believe my eyes; cars, loads of them, were parked all the way along, as far as I could see. Excitedly I looked at Anna. 'Have you seen all the cars? Wow. I can't believe that many people wanted to come. It's so amazing!'

'I told you!' Anna replied, a big grin across her face. 'People love open days. It's a good time to get new volunteers; we usually get loads of offers to help. It's a beautiful day too, which is a bonus.'

The open day was Anna's idea. She'd worked at the animal centre for several years and had always helped organise the event with the previous manager. It was all new to me though, so I had been a bit nervous about how it would go. Looking at the cars, and at the queue which was now forming at the gate, my nerves disappeared, and I couldn't wait until opening time.

It was also Anna's idea to stand at the gate with buckets for members of the public to throw their small change into if they wanted. Marie volunteered straight away. 'I'll put some coins in and shake it all about to encourage them. Kelley will help me, won't you kid?' she asked my daughter, who was hanging off Marie's arm as usual.

'Can I, Mummy? I'll put some coins in too, and shake it all about.' She idolised Marie.

'As long as you don't ask people for money I don't mind. And you mustn't go on the road. And remember to say thank you if someone puts money in your bucket …'

'Okay – okay!' Marie interrupted me. 'Don't panic, lady – I'll look after her! Come on then, let's go find a couple of buckets to shake.' Marie grabbed Kelley, and threw the five-year-old onto her shoulders before taking off up the hill to the kennels.

I looked at Anna. 'Thanks for all your help with this. I'd never have had the courage to do it myself, not in my first year here, and probably not after that either!' I squeezed her arm.

'Oh, give over, you silly old cow,' she said gruffly, and walked off.

On the dot of eleven, Marie opened the main gate, and the people poured in, most of them with change ready to be dropped into the buckets.

The next couple of hours flew by, with people asking questions about the centre and the animals that were currently there. As Anna had said, many of them offered to become volunteers in some way; home-checking or dog walking, with a couple even wanting to help with the cleaning. One lady wanted to play with the cats once a week; and another wanted to help tame any nasty rabbits. All offers were very gratefully accepted, and names and phone numbers written down.

I was totally engrossed in a conversation about leaving money to the RSPCA in a will, when Marie called me to the phone. 'Sorry, Jane, it's about a manky cat. I think someone is going to have to go and collect it.'

I took the receiver from her. 'Hello, I'm Jane; you've found a cat?'

'Hello. Yes – well, no. It found me. It's sitting in my living room right now. Can you come and get it?'

'Is there any way you could bring it in to us? We're in the middle of an open day here.'

'I would if I could, but I can't drive yet, and the parents are away at the moment. Hey, I'm sorry to call you, but it's a bit of a mess. Our Persians won't go into the living room because it smells so bad.'

Why? Why now. A stray cat that the Persians won't go near because it 'smells so bad' is hardly an emergency, is it? I thought angrily.

'The open day finishes at four; could I collect it straight after?' It was a last-ditch attempt.

'Jeez, sounds like I'm being really awkward here, but I have to go out, sorry.'

My heart sank as I realised there was no choice; I'd have to go and collect it. It sank a bit further when I was told the address; it was about twenty miles away, and meant that I was likely to be out for the whole afternoon. *Damn. Damn. And damn.*

Frustrated at having to miss the rest of my first open day, I threw the piece of paper with the address onto the passenger seat next to me and, revving unnecessarily, lurched off.

It wasn't the easiest of places to find; along a tiny road across the South Downs, down a narrow track through a wood, third fork left, second driveway on the right. I got lost trying to find the tiny road across the downs, and arrived almost two hours later.

'I'm so sorry, I followed your directions but got lost on the downs,' I said as I grabbed the cat basket out of the van.

'That's okay. I couldn't go and leave it. I'm in a band – supposed to be getting ready for a gig, but I told my mates that I couldn't make it yet. I can call them in a minute. Come in; the cat's in here.'

I looked around me as I walked into the house. The huge stairway curving gracefully up to the balcony that overlooked the hall, the bronze bust of a long-gone gentleman, the enormous oil paintings that adorned the walls – the place smacked of opulence. I could understand the young lad's concern about a smelly cat in the living room. As I entered that room, my trainers sank into the carpet, and I looked in awe at a beautifully carved cabinet and a brown leather and dark oak suite. Then I noticed the smell; it was foul, and made me want to vomit.

'THAT'S disgusting,' I said, as I followed the young lad through to the other side of the room.

'Oh my God …' I stared at the cat.

It had a wide head, indicating that it was an unneutered male. Its fur was ginger, but sparse. Its skin was full of little holes, round ones, going right through to the muscle and sinew. From almost every hole, maggots fell onto the plush, cream-coloured carpet. The cat's mouth was slightly open, and maggots crawled around inside, disappearing and reappearing under its tongue and around its teeth. Inside its tattered ears were yet more maggots, all jostling each other for the small space deep inside the cat's ears.

'You can see why I called you then,' the lad said quietly.

I had sunk to my knees, but looked up at him when he spoke. 'I've never seen anything like it.' I was too shocked to cry even. The cat sat upright, with a dignity that belied the pain and discomfort it must really have been feeling. Without any struggle, the cat allowed me to pick it up, and lower it into the basket.

I looked at the lad. 'You didn't mention the maggots on the phone,' I accused him. 'I'd never have asked you to wait until after our open day if you'd said about the maggots.'

He was leaning on an arm chair, with his back to me, and moved only to wipe his arm across his face. The sound of his voice told me that he was crying.

'I couldn't. It was hard enough as it was; if I'd tried to say about them ... well ... I couldn't have. Hey, I feel like a right wally as it is. I'm in a rock band, you know ...' He finally turned round.

Guilt washed over me as I looked at his face – he was just a teenager. 'Yes – I do know, and I'm sorry. What can I say, except thank you. You could have just put it outside and left him to it.'

'No I couldn't. There's something about him, I can't put my finger on it. The way he sits there, like it's his lot. It got to me. It's like he came in to our house for a reason; like he wanted help.' The lad blushed. 'Oh, I don't know. Look – I have to go ...'

'Yes of course. Thanks for calling us, and I'll let you know what happens, that's if you want me to? By the way – what's your name?'

'Samuel, but I'm called Sam. I'd like to know how he gets on – I think.'

'Well, thanks again, Sam. Bye.'

In the enclosed space of the van the smell was even worse, and I retched until it mingled with the breeze from the open windows, making the long drive more bearable. I'd already called the vet from a phone box, and he would be waiting for me, so with my foot as far down on the accelerator as I could safely push it, I rattled off down the road.

'This is probably the worst case of maggot infestation I've seen in a cat,' the vet said calmly, as he prodded and poked at the mouth, and ears. 'Enteritis; hence the sickly smell. The wounds are also infected. There may well be an underlying problem that's not instantly obvious. He's dehydrated; emaciated. And those little devils are going to take some getting rid of.'

The vet scraped at the maggots in the cat's left ear, and several fell onto the examination table. He squashed them with a piece of tissue covering his fingers, muttering 'bloody maggots' as they popped under the pressure.

'I can take some blood samples – run some tests – depends how much you want to spend.' He looked at me expectantly.

'What would you do?' I always asked him for his opinion.

'There could be, and probably is, an underlying problem, but a couple of tests won't break the RSPCA bank. I'm not convinced that he'll make it – but I expect you'll want to try. I'd give it a go. You've got little to lose; he's got everything to gain.'

'If there's even a slight chance, I want to give it to him.' I always found it difficult to control my voice when I had this sort of conversation with him, and tried to keep it short.

'Good. Right then.' The vet busied himself drawing up several syringes of hope, before plunging them into the lean body. 'If this cocktail doesn't make him feel better, nothing will. I'll give you some sachets of Lectade to put in his water. If he doesn't drink, you must syringe it into him. Boiled chicken only, to start, anything else will be too rich. Clear up the enteritis and rehydrate him, or he won't make it.'

I watched as he carefully pulled maggots out of the cat's left ear with a pair of tweezers, plucking out several each time, and dropping them into a bowl, and when he couldn't reach any more, he patiently started on the right ear.

'You must bear in mind that they are eating him, and the longer they stay in there, the more damage they are likely to be doing down inside those ears; time will tell how much. But I'm sure you won't rest until they're all gone.' He smiled at me, and as the lump in my throat prevented me from speaking, I nodded.

'Antibiotic cream. You must rub this into the wounds twice a day. It should help.' He smiled again. 'Good luck. If he's alive in three days I'd like to see him.' I nodded again.

I made up a comfy bed in the cat isolation unit, with a thick, woollen jumper I'd found in a bag of jumble that had been donated to us. Then I boiled up a chicken leg, and stirred the rehydration powder into a small bowl of water.

The cat sat, upright, in the bed, just as it had on the living room carpet, and allowed me to syringe 20ml of the fluid into his mouth.

Much to my disappointment he ignored the chicken, so I cut it into the tiniest of pieces and mixed it up with some of the water. With a bit stuck on the end of my finger, I opened his mouth and wiped some of the mix onto the inside of his cheek. A maggot, almost half an inch long, crawled across his tongue and stuck to the bits left on my finger, before wriggling free and falling onto the woolly jumper. It burrowed into the wool immediately, so I grabbed the jumper and squeezed the bit where the maggot was. I grinned as I felt it pop.

The cat swallowed the mix, so I carried on, bit by bit, until he'd eaten about a teaspoonful. It wasn't much, but I was forcing his mouth open each time, and didn't want to hurt or upset him.

Every morning he let me weigh him. He didn't need to go into a cat basket – he sat upright on the scales without moving. Every four hours during the day and evening, I hand fed him the chicken mix, and syringed the Lectade into him. Twice every day I smothered him in antibiotic cream. I borrowed my Dad's magnifying glass, and plucked a maggot from the depths of his ears whenever I saw one. I stroked his cheeks, the only part of his body not covered in holes or cream. And as the hours passed into days, my heartstrings tugged towards him more and more.

After three days, he was still alive. The enteritis had stopped, and I'd dug out the last maggots, purely because they had grown big enough to grab with the tweezers.

The cat sat, upright as usual, on the examination table once again.

'My, my, what a difference.' He inserted the tip of an auriscope into the cat's left ear. 'No maggots; and no infection that I can see. Good.'

Into the right ear. 'No maggots, but a bit of inflammation, I'll give you some drops to put in.'

'He hasn't put on any weight, but he hasn't lost any either,' I told the vet as he looked into the cat's mouth. 'He's eating the chicken out of the bowl now, so I'm hoping his weight will improve. Could I give him anything else to eat as well?'

'Yes, poached fish; not smoked. They usually like cod. And you can mash it up with a very small amount of well cooked rice; see if he'll take it. Good. I'm pleased with his progress.'

The cat didn't murmur when I added the ear drops to the daily routine. And when I gently rubbed the ear to make the drops go in as far as possible, he inclined his head towards me, just a tiny bit. He seemed to enjoy the poached fish and rice, and his appetite increased gradually, until he was eating reasonable amounts, including tinned cat food, which the vet had suggested slowly introducing into his diet.

The blood test results arrived and showed nothing major, so I decided it was safe to give the cat a name. I called him Samson.

'Hello Sam, it's Jane from the RSPCA. I just wanted to let you know how the cat is doing.' Happily, I told Sam how things were, and he was chuffed. He told me he'd asked his parents if he could have the cat – if it lived. I admit, I heaved a sigh of relief when he said they'd refused. I loved all animals, but dogs had always been my real passion – until now. Now, my heart had been well and truly captured by this dignified, unassuming cat; and he wasn't going anywhere.

All but two of Samson's wounds had healed, and I was plastering the cream on one of them when he put his paw, gently, onto my arm, and looked at me. I stopped, but didn't move. 'Bless you, Samson,' I said, and a lump grew in my throat as I stroked his ears.

'Anna – he put his paw on my arm!' I shouted across the animal centre when I caught sight of her through the window. She came over and looked at him.

'He must be feeling better, poor little bugger.' She stroked his head. 'I wonder if he's ever been shown any affection. He's not one of those aloof cats that don't want to know you, and he's not one of the nasty little bleeders who bite you if you touch them somewhere they don't like.' She scratched him under his chin, and he tilted his head slightly up, to give her better access.

'He's a bit of a mystery,' I answered. 'He accepts all the unpleasant things that I do to him without any fuss. It's strange, but like the young lad, Sam, said: there's definitely something about him.' I touched his ear before closing him into the unit.

On his first visit outdoors in weeks, he didn't surprise me; he sat, upright, and looked around him. I sat next to him, and for a while we watched the world go by. After that, we'd spend time together every day, just sitting and watching. One morning, as I put a fresh bowl of food into his unit, he rubbed his head against my hand. I picked him up and cuddled him, and cried into his fur.

He began to spend his days outside the cattery, when it wasn't raining. He never went anywhere, just sat and watched us all going about our business, and when he'd had enough, he went back into his unit.

I sat there with him, late one evening, absentmindedly stroking his ears while I listened to the crickets, when he put his paw on my hand again. I stopped stroking, and looked at him. He climbed onto my lap, and for the first time, he purred. Bursting with happiness, I picked him up and cuddled him to me. The gentle purring continued, and his front paws pummelled slowly, rhythmically, into my jumper. *This is what my job is all about.* I rested my head against his and we sat for an age, cuddling.

When his purring stopped, I smiled, thinking he'd gone to sleep; until I realised he'd stopped breathing.

'Samson?' Adrenalin pumping like mad, I put my hands around him and lifted him, but his limp little head hung over the side of my arm. My tears mingled with his fur as reality struck me; he was dead. I cried until there were no tears left, and with a thumping headache I wrapped him up in a pale blue, cotton sheet, leaving just his head visible. As I lay him into his bed, I stroked him for the last time and whispered to him, 'Goodbye Samson.'

CHAPTER 9

The Great Escape?

'I hate my job; I'm leaving,' I told Tony as I stood in our kitchen and poured boiling water into his cafetiere.

'You know you don't mean that.' He wrapped his arms around me and gave me a big hug.

I pushed him away. 'Yes. I do mean it. Tony, I spend an inordinately large amount of my time crying because of my job. Why would I want to keep a job that just makes me cry all the time?' I started crying again as I threw a tea bag into my mug.

'You're upset because of Samson, but you'll get over it. You must remember what the vet said; he didn't think the cat would make it.'

I turned on him. 'I remember what the bloody vet said but it doesn't make any difference! My point is – I'd have cried whether Samson made it or not; it's all I ever seem to do. I cry when something goes right because I'm so happy and relieved; and I cry when something goes wrong – because I get so emotionally involved with all the damned animals.' I paused and wiped my eyes on the hanky that Tony held out to me.

In a quieter tone, I continued, 'I don't think I'm cut out for all this shit. I wanted to work for the RSPCA to help animals, and I thought I'd be able to handle the cruelty and suffering that I knew I'd be bound to see sometimes, but I had rose-coloured spectacles on, and they've been well and truly ripped off. You need to have the hide of a bloody rhino to do this job; people don't realise. I don't even eat meat because it would be sacrilege to me. I just can't cope with it any more.' I rushed upstairs, threw myself on the bed, and sobbed. Trix followed, and lay next to me, resting her head across my cheek.

I'd cried myself dry and was sitting on the edge of the bed cuddling Trix when I heard the stairs creak.

'I've made you a cup of tea.'

Without looking up at Tony I muttered, 'Thank you.' My head felt heavy, like I had a really bad cold, and my nose was bunged up.

He continued, 'I've given the girls some cereal and they're watching the TV.'

'Oh God …' I put my head in my hands, 'Edwina's got play school today; I'd better get my act together.' I slurped my steaming tea, and felt a little bit better.

'We need some bread and milk. Do you want me to get it while I'm out?' Tony asked.

'No it's okay, I'll get it. Tony: I love you.'

'I love you too.' He bent down and gave me a big hug, and this time I didn't push him away.

I waved my eldest three off on the school bus, and drove the four miles to play school. Edwina hugged my legs, and I promised to buy her a chocolate bar. She went straight to the six ducklings that had been hatched from eggs and dropped a lemon curd sandwich into their run. She had made it herself, just for them. I smiled; like mother – like daughter, and hoped that for her sake, she didn't turn out as soft as me. The tears welled up in my eyes. *Oh for God's sake …*

Completely preoccupied with my thoughts, I automatically took items from the supermarket shelves and dropped them into the trolley. I found myself in the animal food aisle, where tins of cat food, with pictures of happy, healthy cats, stared at me. One of them was ginger, with a wide face; like Samson's. The usual lump formed in my throat and the usual tears pricked my eyelids, so with my head down, I made for the quietest aisle I could find. Marzipan; I stared through the tears at the packet I'd randomly picked up, and spent an age looking at the foil wrapping.

Anna wasn't around when I got home, which was a relief. I needed to think about how to tell her I'd had enough, and was going to leave. The shopping was heavy; I'd somehow ended up with much more than a loaf of bread and a pint of milk, but I dragged all the bags out of the van together to save me from going outside again.

The dogs knew the sound of my Sherpa, and were all waiting at the back door. They milled around me as I made my way to the kitchen, knowing that as soon as I'd put the shopping away they would get a chocolate biscuit each. As I put the bags on the cupboard, I noticed a big chunk of foam on the floor. Curious, I walked through to the dining room, where several more large chunks lay around. With foreboding, I walked slowly into the living room, and there I found where the foam had come from. The sofa of my brand new, mink velour three-piece suite was in bits, everywhere. Big chunks of foam, small chunks of foam, strips of ripped-up velour and velour-covered buttons with the string still attached were scattered over the entire floor.

Tina, my adorable Collie cross, who was looking up at me from between my legs, waiting patiently for her biscuit, was undoubtedly the culprit.

Tony found me a bit later, crawling around the floor, shoving my sofa into dustbin bags while the tears dripped off my cheeks onto the carpet.

'Here.' He handed me a small cardboard box full of cotton wool, saying nothing about the exposed wooden frame from which strips of material hung like tendrils.

'What's in it?' I wasn't really interested, but I wiped my eyes and grabbed a handful of the cotton wool.

'CAREFUL!' He bent down and cupped his hands underneath the box. 'They're … very fragile.'

Puzzled, I looked up at him before lowering the box down to the carpet. With both hands I pulled the cotton wool apart in the middle and exposed a baby something, which was covered in sawdust.

In wonder, I looked up at Tony. 'What is it?'

'A baby squirrel. Two, in fact. A tree was blown down across a road, and two men went to deal with it. One of them was using a chainsaw and noticed the sawdust moving on the ground under the branch he was cutting. Being curious, he scooped it up, and found these.'

'Oh.' I took one out of the box. Its eyes were still closed, but it moved in little circles around the palm of my hand using its extremely long back legs. Fur had already begun to grow through the pink skin, and the tail, which was the same thickness right to the tip, looked almost as long as its body. Its front feet looked like hands, with long, thin fingers which reminded me of a small monkey.

As I stroked its side, it wriggled around, pushing its nose into my hand.

Tony smiled as he watched. 'Strange little thing, isn't it? The vet has checked them both and they're fine. He says they must be more than five days old because of the growth of fur, and less than ten days old because their eyes are still closed. He's given me some powdered milk for them, and a bottle and teats.' Tony held up the bottle. 'I take it you want to give them a chance? Or are you still leaving? If you are I …'

'Oh shut up.'

Tina had been sitting behind the coffee table since I'd started putting my sofa into rubbish bags. She'd watched my every move, and wagged the tip of her tail each time I looked over at her, but didn't dare come near me after I'd yelled at her for what she'd done. Now, she sidled over and sniffed at my cupped hands, trying to put her nose in the gap between them.

'You can sod off,' I said to her, but she could tell by the tone of my voice that I didn't mean it, and shoved her nose in a little more. When it touched the tail she stopped, and sniffed for several seconds before gently licking it.

'Look at her, Tony – she just licked its tail!' I opened up my hands to show Tony, and Tina got straight down to business, giving its bum a good clean. I was fascinated when it did a wee as she licked, but winced when it pooed and she lapped it up.

'Looks like you've got a surrogate mum there.' Tony handed me the bottle and teats. 'The powdered milk is on the kitchen cupboard. I've got a lot of calls to make so I'll see you later.' He blew me a kiss as he went.

I knew nothing about hand-rearing baby anythings, and immediately felt the weight of their little lives on my shoulders. *Oh, woman – what have you let yourself in for this time …?*

It was one thing mixing up powdered milk and putting it in a bowl for a cat to lap up as a few lumps didn't matter – but entirely another mixing it up to the correct consistency and putting it in a tiny glass bottle, with a rubber teat about one inch long and no wider than a drinking straw.

In my haste to get some milk into them, I didn't read the instructions properly, and with the milk in the bottle, and the teat wedged as tightly onto the glass end as I could get it, I opened the squirrel's mouth and inserted the teat. It pushed the teat around with its tongue, but no milk came out. The flow of milk was controlled by putting a thumb over the hole at the other end of the bottle, so I removed my thumb and jiggled the bottle around a bit, but still no milk came out. *Hmm, so how the hell do you get the milk to come out of the teat then?* I put the squirrel back into the box, and squeezed the teat between my fingers. Still nothing. *Oh for God's sake* … It took me a while to work out that the teat didn't have a hole in it.

Following the instructions to the letter, I cut off the tip of the teat, picked up one of the babies and pushed the teat into its mouth, leaving a tiny gap at the end of the bottle with my thumb. The squirrel could obviously smell the milk this time and frantically moved its head around, trying to suck the teat. At last it latched on. *Yey! This is the way to do it.* I grinned with delight; I was feeding a baby squirrel! But within seconds the squirrel started choking and I watched in horror as milk splurted out of its mouth and nose and it fought for breath. *Oh God ... this is not supposed to happen.*

In a complete panic, I grabbed some toilet roll and mopped its face. *Oh God ... what HAVE I done ...?*

To my enormous relief, the sneezing and gasping eventually stopped, and the baby squirrel started to breathe properly again, so with a trembling hand, I put the milk-soaked little thing back into the box. *Okay, stop. Have a cigarette. Think.*

Tony was always having to sew up his trouser pockets, and kept a good supply of different sized needles in a tin. I chose one of the thicker ones, and using my lighter, warmed up the end of the needle until it burned red, then I quickly shoved the burning needle through the tip of a new teat until it had gone right through to the inside. *Looking good – looking gooood ...*

I sucked the teat myself this time, to make sure that it actually worked, and grimaced at the taste of the burnt rubber.

With the freshly washed teat on the end of the bottle, and the milk once more slightly heated, I got a squirrel out of the box and put the bottle to its mouth.

I watched in amazement, as the squirrel sucked like there was no tomorrow and the milk slowly disappeared. The baby finally lay still in the palm of my hand, with an enormous, bulging belly, sated. I looked in awe at this tiny creature, which twitched in its sleep as I gently touched its front paw, and felt the usual lump form in the back of my throat.

'Dare I ask how they are doing?' Tony said, as soon as he got home that evening.

'They're doing really well. I've had to draw up a rota to stop the girls from arguing about who feeds them next.' I pointed to the fridge door.

'They know the squirrels might die,' I continued, 'I've told them straight.' *And I've told myself too ...*

He pulled me to him. 'And how about you? Are you okay now?'

I looked at him. 'Yes, I'm okay now. I don't know if I will ever harden up, but I do know I wouldn't want to do anything else.'

He took my hand and kissed it. 'That's what I was hoping to hear.'

'MUMMY. LISA SAID IT'S SIX O'CLOCK. I'VE GOT TO FEED THE SQUIRRELS,' shouted Shanie from the living room.

'OKAY. WON'T BE A MINUTE.' I put the kettle on to make the milk.

Watching my five-year-old daughter as I helped her feed the babies, I realised how lucky we all were; there couldn't be many children this privileged. Shanie didn't move until it was bed time, for the squirrels had been snuggled up in her long hair at the back of her neck.

Two days later their eyes opened, so we guessed they were now ten days old. They were already exploring their little box, but now that they could see, they tried to climb over the six-inch sides.

'Oi!' I shrieked, laughing, as one of them actually managed to climb over, and land on the table with a tiny thud. 'What do you think you're doing then, eh? Come on you little so-and-so.' I scooped him up and he tried to suckle from one of my fingers as I put him back into the box. No sooner was he back in, than he climbed out again. This time, Tony caught him as he dropped.

'Tony, we know nothing about rearing baby animals.' I watched as the squirrel clambered across his hands. 'How do you wean a baby squirrel? What do you feed it? How old should it be when you start to wean it?'

I grabbed the other baby as it balanced precariously on the top edge of the cardboard box. 'Can you ring Head-quarters and get some advice? Surely someone there must know what to do.'

'I should think so. They've got all the different depart-ments; there must be one that can help. I'll give them a call in the morning.'

I took the baby from him and it climbed up my jumper and round to the back of my neck. I didn't have long hair for it to nestle in, so it climbed inside my jumper instead, and slept on my shoulder while I went to the summer house and found a hamster cage to put their box in. Along the way I picked up a stick and wedged it into the wire for the squirrels to climb on. I put their box sideways into the cage and watched them as they haltingly exploring their new home.

It was my job to feed them before bed, and it was one of my favourite times. As always, Tina was there, her nose rest-ing gently on my knees while she waited to give the young-sters a good clean. As I held the bottle up, the baby grabbed at it, and for the first time managed to wrap its front paws around the teat as it guzzled the milk down. I had to tug the empty bottle out of its mouth to refill it, but after drinking half the second bottle, its eyes began to close and it eventually stopped sucking. It didn't move as I pulled my fingers from around its body; just lay, with its back legs spread out behind, belly flat on the towel, and slept. Tina's nose crept forward and she whined quietly, so I lowered the baby towards her. As I watched my oh-so-naughty dog carefully clean it from top to bottom, I felt the usual tug of the heartstrings, the prick of tears. I was bursting with love and happiness.

'Right,' said Tony, the next morning. 'I phoned HQ and they gave me a couple of numbers of people who take in orphaned and injured wildlife. I've just spoken to someone, and they said as soon as the squirrels reach three weeks, start giving them the dried, fruit-flavoured baby food, mixed up with water, and put it on a saucer so that they can get right into it. They also like the dried baby rice, brown bread, grapes, apples and perhaps a bit of broccoli to nibble on. That should do for starters. When they're a bit older we can add rabbit mix and nuts in shells.'

'Well that's easy then. You can get that lot on your way home later.'

Tony continued, 'Unfortunately, there is a problem; a very big problem.'

'Oh no; has your van broken down?'

'No, I don't mean that sort of problem. HQ has also told me that it's illegal to release grey squirrels back into the wild.'

'What?' I looked at him. 'You are joking? They've just come from the wild for Christ's sake – what do you mean, they can't be released again?'

'I mean – they can't be released once they've been reared. They have to stay in captivity for the rest of their lives. Apparently grey squirrels are not indigenous to this country, they were brought here by landowners in the nineteenth century.'

'What the hell has all that got to do with anything? Rabbits weren't from here originally either; they were brought in by the Romans in some past and distant century, but they can be released. How bloody stupid.' I grabbed my cigarette packet off the table and pulled two out, throwing one at Tony and lighting my own.

'Getting angry won't do you any good. If it's the law, then it's the law; there's nothing we can do about it.' Tony stood up. 'I'll get that food and bring it home later then.' He leaned down and gave me a peck on the cheek.

Bloody ridiculous rules and regulations. What the hell difference is it going to make to the world if I release you? I blew my smoke up into the air as I watched one of the babies try, yet again, to climb onto the stick. *If your tree hadn't fallen down you wouldn't be here anyway, you'd have been reared by your own parents and no-one would have even known you existed.* The baby finally made it and was soon joined by its sibling, who balanced precariously for a few moments before falling off. Not to be deterred, it got straight up and tried again. As I watched them both, dangling from their stick, I was incensed by the unfairness of it all.

'Hi.' I stopped stirring the delicious-smelling stew my mum had made for our tea, and gave Tony a loving kiss as he walked through the kitchen door that evening. 'The girls want to name the squirrels, but I don't know if we should.' Thoughts of Samson came to me, and I unreasonably felt that the squirrels had a better chance of surviving if we didn't call them anything.

'They even agreed on names without arguing – Tom and Jerry. What do you think?'

'Mm, I think that's a good choice.' He smiled as Lisa walked between us with a squirrel sitting on each shoulder. Tina followed closely behind, eager to carry out the next bum cleaning session.

'Are we mad?' I asked Tony, as Lisa got a loaf of brown bread, pulled a chunk out of the soft middle, gave a bit to each of the squirrels, chucked the rest to Tina, then walked back out again.

'Yes,' Tony answered.

'I thought so.' I carried on stirring the stew.

By the age of three weeks, Tom and Jerry were lapping up their fruit-flavoured baby food and climbing everywhere. They loved clawing their way up the velvet curtains in the living room, and the pelmet was a favourite with its gold tassels hanging all the way along. But they often misjudged as they tried to leap from one tassel to another, and whenever they ended up on the floor, Tina was ready and waiting to scoop them up by their scruffs and take them to her bed.

An ever constant battle ensued between them; Tina wanted to mother them, and they wanted to explore. No sooner had Tina settled down with one of them, than it was off – up over the side of her rib cage, onto the back of her wicker bed and then straight up the curtain. More often than not, the brother would already be on the floor by this time, and so Tina would start all over again. I actually felt quite sorry for her, and decided it was time for the boys to move outside.

'Can you build a run then?' I asked Tony when he came home that evening. 'They are old enough to go outside now surely?'

Tony watched them leaping along the top of the pelmet. 'Yes, I'd say they were old enough now. I've got some wood; I could try and build one under the hazelnut tree up next to the top dog run. That way I could possibly incorporate one of the branches in it to make it more natural for them.'

'Oh, that's a great idea! There are loads of hazelnuts growing on it, I only looked a couple of days ago because I wanted to cut one of the branches to put in their run, but your idea is much better. Can you start it tomorrow?'

Tony looked over his glasses at me. 'I thought we were going out for lunch tomorrow?'

'Oh I know, but this is more important. They are running Tina ragged and it's not fair to any of them. She wants to smother them, and they want to explore. I feel really guilty now when I put them back into their cage, but I can't leave them out all the time. And they've started running all over the place; I found one in the bathroom this morning, and the window was open so it could easily have escaped.'

'Okay, I'll start it tomorrow, but it will take a couple of days at least. And I will need some fine mesh wire, probably a whole roll of it.'

'Thanks love.' I smiled at him. 'I can't wait to see what they think of their new home.'

Almost two rolls of wire mesh, and a lot more wood than Tony had wanted to use, later, I stood back and beamed at the huge run I'd encouraged my husband to build. Half the trunk, and two large branches of the hazel nut tree were incorporated, and there was plenty of room for humans to stand upright, and walk around inside.

'Did I ever tell you how much I love you?' I hugged Tony as I continued to admire the new structure. 'It's bloody amazing – really, it's like a squirrel palace. They are going to love it. Thank you, thank you, thank you.'

'I must admit, I'm quite pleased with the way it's turned out, although the wire is a bit messy around the trunk, but it was difficult to make sure there were no sharp ends inside the run.' He opened the door, which was about a foot from the ground, and only just big enough for him to get through, and squeezed his way in. 'I made the door small so that they are less likely to be able to escape when anyone enters. I should have made a double door but we'd have needed more materials, so you will just have to be careful.'

'The door is great, and we will be careful.' I followed him around as he examined his work for a final time. I hadn't realised that he was capable of building something like this so well, and I was over the moon. 'So – as soon as the girls get back from Mum's, can we bring Tom and Jerry out?'

'I suppose so. I think it's secure; at least, I can't find any holes or gaps.' He squeezed back out through the door. 'It'll be interesting to see what they make of it.'

Part of the run was covered with corrugated sheeting to keep out the rain and wind, so I placed the hamster cage on a small wooden platform that Tony had made for it, and opened the door. Both squirrels leapt out straight away, but once on top of the cage, didn't move. They sat, sniffing the air for several seconds, then suddenly they were off.

Tony put his arm around me as we watched them run effortlessly up the side of the trunk and along the highest branch. They both stopped, and one of them cleaned his front paws, but the other took off into the air. I gasped, and closed my eyes; there was no soft carpet or sofa for them to land on when they missed now.

'Wow! Did you see that!' shouted Lisa.

I opened my eyes again, to see that he'd landed safely on the very end of the lower branch, and was dangling upside down as he crawled through the leaves.

It was like watching a firework display, with shrieks of delight from the girls every few seconds as the squirrels became more and more daring. When they were both finally worn out, they took themselves off to their hamster cage, and went to bed.

Tony smiled at me as we walked, arm in arm, back indoors. 'I think it's safe to say they like their new home.'

'I think you are absolutely right. It's so good to see them in a more natural environment. Shame that they have to stay contained though; and totally unfair.'

'Now don't start that again.' Tony pulled me to him and looked at me. 'You know how it has to be and there's no point in fretting about it; the law is the law.' He kissed me on the end of my nose.

'I know, I know, but it doesn't mean I have to be happy about it. It's a stupid law, but okay, I shan't say any more about it, I shall make coffee instead.'

'You shan't say any more about it?' Tony raised his eyebrows. 'For how long – an hour or two?'

'Well it's a bloody daft law, Tony, we both know that.'

'Tut tut. I thought you weren't going to say any more about it?'

'Stop winding me up and I'll shut up, okay?' I pretended to glare at him.

'That'll be the day.'

I threw a tea bag at him, missing by several feet.

Much to the annoyance of my daughters, I stopped all human contact with Tom and Jerry over a period of weeks. The girls remonstrated daily at first, unable to understand why I wouldn't let them go into the run any more, but I couldn't tell them why I wanted the squirrels to be as wild as possible – I couldn't tell anyone.

'MUMMY! MUMMY! THE SQUIRRELS HAVE GOT OUT!' shouted Edwina as she ran down towards me. 'QUICKLY MUMMY – THEY'RE RUNNING AROUND IN THE TREE!' she finished as she rushed back up the hill again.

Tony looked straight at me.

'What? WHAT?' I responded. My face burned red as I returned his stare.

Without another word, he marched up to the squirrel run and examined it thoroughly. I dragged along behind.

'So – how did they make this hole?' He'd pushed his hand through a gap between the trunk and the wire. 'Well?'

I looked at the ground. *Sod it – he knows me too well.*

Tony squeezed back out through the door and took both my elbows in his hands. Sheepishly, I looked up at his stern, serious looking face, and waited for the onslaught.

'Janie, I love you.' He put his arms around me and kissed me hard on the lips.

With huge relief, I returned his kiss, and as I looked up into the tree, saw Tom and Jerry, sitting on a small piece of wood I'd nailed onto one of the highest branches to use as a feeding station, cracking open Brazil nuts.

Grinning from ear to ear was quite difficult while being passionately kissed, but I managed.

CHAPTER 10

Anyone for Tea?

'Can we take in a four-month-old castrated male goat?' Anna asked.

'Another one? What is it with people and goats at the moment?' We had only recently taken in five-year-old Crystal, a big, brown crossbred goat, and two-year-old Heineken, a castrated Pygmy, with a huge fat belly and stumpy legs. 'What's the problem then?'

'He keeps escaping and running off next door, where he eats the neighbour's plants. Apparently the owners have already had to pay out quite a bit in compensation for various shrubs and fruit bushes. He's even eaten all the bark off a young plum tree. Today, he walked through the greenhouse – literally – and ate most of the plants. What he didn't eat, he knocked over and trampled. He's lucky he didn't get hurt because he's broken several panes of glass too. The people next door have had enough and are threatening all sorts of things if the owners don't do something to stop him, but they don't know how he gets out, so they don't know what they can do. The lady's at her wits' end. Yes?' Anna looked at me expectantly, already knowing the answer.

'Yes.'

She grinned at me as she told the owner we would collect the goat that afternoon.

'Isn't he gorgeous!' said Marie, as she shoved his head, pretending to butt him. The new goat swaggered closer to her and pushed her hand with his head, totally unperturbed at the fact that he'd just spent the last half an hour travelling in the back of my van.

'He wants to play! Can we have him, Mum?' she asked Anna, as she offered the youngster a bunch of dandelion leaves.

'No you bloody can't. Where on earth would we keep a goat? Anyway, I expect he's been lonely, being all on his own since he was a few weeks old, and that's probably why he keeps escaping. The people got him because they thought he would eat all the weeds and save them some digging. His name's Dexter, by the way.'

By the next morning it was as if Dexter had been with us for years. As I collected their food bowls to give them breakfast, he pranced around Heineken, trying to get the older goat to play. When Heineken gave him a good butt in the side and bowled him over, he jumped straight up and went back for more. Crystal came over to eat, but neither of the boys bothered; they were too busy running up and down the paddock together. As I walked away, I knew that if we did re-home them they would have to go together.

Later that morning, Anna poked her head round the cattery door. 'Any idea where the tea bags are?'

On my knees, I finished sweeping the last of the cat litter into the dustpan. 'On the cupboard, by the kettle; or they should be. Is it that time already?' I stood up and stretched. 'Don't kittens make a bloody mess with the litter? They've scattered all the clean stuff everywhere. It's taken me ages to sweep it all up again.'

As I spoke, a kitten leapt up and hooked its claws into the skin just above my knee. 'OW – OW – OW!' I grabbed the kitten and, one at a time, removed its claws from my leg. 'You little horror!' I tickled its ears and it immediately started biting my hand playfully.

'Time wasters. That's what kittens are.' Anna laughed. 'You could easily spend all day in there, playing with them as well as cleaning up behind them.'

'And as well as pulling their claws out of you,' I added, as I put the kitten on the floor. 'He's done that to me a few times now. Seems to think my legs are some sort of climbing frame.' As I opened the cat-run door to leave, he shot past me and leapt up the wire in the corridor.

'Ha-ha! You won't get out of here that easily.' I extricated the kitten from the wire on the ceiling as he hung tight with just his front paws, and put him back into his run before following Anna to the staff kitchen.

I looked inside all the cupboards, but couldn't find the tea bags. 'Hmm, I know I put them back this morning. Oh well, I'll go indoors and get some.' I scooted off to my own kitchen and grabbed a handful.

'These are for you.' I wrinkled my nose as I gave Anna a plateful of pig's trotter sandwiches. 'My mum's cooked loads of them; my kitchen smells disgusting.'

'Oooo! Your mum is a love, isn't she?' Anna drooled over the plateful of feet.

'I don't know how you lot can eat the hairy toes of a pig.'
I looked at the pile of fat and skin protruding from between
the pieces of bread, and shuddered as I went to make the tea.

Several days later, Anna came and found me in the
summer house. 'Have you seen the tea bags?'

'On the cupboard, by the kettle, or at least they should be.'
I looked at her. 'Am I having a déjà vu moment? I know I put
them back this morning; I'm sure I did …

We both looked in all the cupboards but couldn't find the
tea bags, so I went indoors and got some more.

About a week later I went into the kitchen to make the tea.
As I picked up the kettle, I noticed the empty spot next to it,
and realised that the tea bags were gone, again. 'Anna, the tea
bags have gone again.'

'This is weird,' she answered. 'How many times have they
gone missing now?'

'I think this is the third time. Right. I'm going to get some
more, but we'll have to keep them inside the cupboard from
now on. We've gone through hundreds over the last couple
of weeks.'

No more tea bags disappeared from the staff kitchen.

A couple of months later, I was indoors, and went to make
a cup of tea. The tea bags, which in my kitchen were kept on
the work surface next to the kettle, were gone. I did a double
take, but they still weren't there. *Where are they?* I searched
around, but didn't find them. *What the hell is going on around
here?* I went outside and saw Anna.

'My tea bags have gone.'

'Oh no. That's spooky. It's been months, hasn't it? I wonder
why it's happened again.' We looked at each other in silence.

When my tea bags disappeared again two days later, I almost freaked. 'Tony; it's scary. The tea bags just go. There's no way anyone is coming indoors and taking them, and yet they go.'

'I must admit it's strange. Keep the back door shut, and put the tea bags inside the cupboard instead and we'll see what happens.'

'I've already done that. It worked when we put them inside the cupboard in the staff kitchen, but the thing is – it's damn scary.' I'd never felt uncomfortable in the cottage before, but I certainly did now.

A week or so later, I walked past my back door, and it was open when I'd left it shut. With trepidation I walked through the door and quietly leaned round the frame into the kitchen. The cupboard door was open – the tea bags gone. Trembling, and in a state of shock, I went and found Anna.

'My … back door was open … My … cupboard door was open … My tea bags were …'

'NO! Don't tell me. Gone.' She gaped at me.

I nodded.

'Christ – this is silly.' Anna said.

'This is scary, Anna,' I responded. 'I don't even want to go into my own kitchen now.'

'I really don't blame you.' She squeezed my arm. 'Come and have a cuppa with me.'

The next day, I was sitting on the floor of the summer house, brushing a rabbit. Anna had taken a dog for a walk in the field next door, and with no visitors looking around, the remaining dogs all lay quietly in their outside runs, most of them snoozing in the afternoon sun. I was daydreaming about Christmas presents I wanted to buy for my girls when I heard the latch go on my back door. I stiffened and slowly turned, not wanting to look but having to, and there was Dexter, standing on his hind legs and shoving the latch up with his nose.

In disbelief I watched as he got down and pushed the bottom part of the stable type door with his head, then walked into my kitchen. I dashed down and peeped through the window just in time to see him push his nose through the tiniest gap between the cupboard doors and flick one of them open with the side of his head. As it rebounded, he pushed forward and it bounced off his left shoulder. He leaned into the cupboard, got the tea bag box between his teeth and pulled it out. A tea bag fell out as the box landed on the floor, and Dexter immediately picked it up and ate it.

It took him a few attempts to get a good grip on the box with his teeth, but once he had, he loped off down to the main gate. Panicked, I ran after him, thinking he was going to get out, as the gate was open, but he stopped before he reached it and squeezed through the smallest of holes in the privet hedge surrounding my front garden. The hedge was at least two and a half feet wide, and as I stared in after him, I saw a few tea bags on the ground, some which looked like they'd been there for months and some which looked quite fresh.

As I pulled my head out of the hedge, Anna walked past me with a quizzical expression on her face. I grinned at her as I ran round to my garden gate and got through it just in time to see Dexter disappear into the hedge on the far side, which separated his paddock from my garden. I couldn't help giggling as I ran round to the paddock, and there I found Dexter and Heineken munching tea bags.

'ANNA – QUICK – GOAT PADDOCK!'

Within seconds Anna appeared.

'What on earth is going on?' she puffed, as she reached my side.

I pointed into the paddock. 'Look.'

I watched her face as realisation hit her.

'The little sods, how the hell do they do it?' she said, and we both burst out laughing. I explained what I'd seen.

Crystal wandered over to see what all the fuss was about, but refused the tea bag that I offered her. As she leaned her side against the fence and rubbed backwards and forwards, I scratched all along her spine. 'What I'd like to know is – what do they do with the box? I've never seen a tea bag box around anywhere, otherwise I might have twigged what was going on.'

'That's what they do,' said Anna, pointing to Heineken. He'd had enough of the tea bags, and picking up the box, he shook it until the bit in his mouth tore off. Within seconds, he'd eaten it. Dexter hoovered up the bags as they flew out of the box, and in a matter of minutes, there wasn't a shred of evidence left.

'Would you believe it?' I turned to Anna. 'Would you bloody believe it?'

'Since I've worked here, Jane, I'd believe anything. I must admit though, that was a bit of a surprise. The good thing is, you can stop worrying about who keeps stealing the tea bags now.'

'Oh God – to think I was actually scared, and it was just a *goat ...*' I groaned, thinking of the way I'd freaked out about my tea bags going missing.

Tony put a wire fence along the inside of the privet hedge, and I changed my daily routine. Instead of giving the goats their usual dry mix every day for breakfast, I did a detour to the kitchen, got a handful of tea bags, and sprinkled them liberally onto the goat mix, and from that day, the tea bags never went missing from the kitchens again.

CHAPTER 11

Justice for Rocky

Tony was agitated when he opened the office door. 'I need your help; now. I've just been on a call-out to a dog, and it isn't looking too good. There's another dog at the property and it won't let me into the garden.'

'Anna's off today; there's only me here.'

'Can you ring her?' he asked.

'Well, I suppose I can. Is it that serious?'

'Yes it is.'

Knowing my husband the way I did, he wouldn't be exaggerating; I rang Anna. Bless her – she said she'd be there within fifteen minutes.

'What's it about then?' I asked Tony as we drove along.

'I had a call about an extremely thin dog which lives in a garden. Today it had difficulty walking, and fell over several times while the neighbours watched. Another dog lives at the premises, usually inside, although lately it's been out all the time as well. The owners haven't been seen for several days now.

'When I get there, I knock on the door but there's no answer, so I go and look round the back. A dog, looks like it's a German Shepherd cross, is lying in the garden, not moving. I open the back gate to get in to it, but the other dog, which also looks like a German Shepherd cross, keeps leaping up at me. It might well be friendly, but judging by the amount of snapping and snarling going on, I'm not so sure.'

'So – what do you want me to do when we get there?' I asked.

'I've got two graspers. If we can try and get the dog on at least one of them, I can hold onto it while you go in and look at the other dog. Once we know if the dog is alive, I can decide what action to take.'

'Okay.' I nodded, a bit surprised about the turn of events. I often accompanied Tony when he was called out at night to attend injured badgers and foxes, and I'd become quite adept at crawling through brambles, thistles and stinging nettles, but I'd never been involved in anything like this before.

The neighbours that had originally called were waiting outside the front of the house when we pulled up and the woman went straight round to Tony.

'He still hasn't moved. We're so worried about him.' She looked across the van at her husband. 'We should have called earlier. I knew we should have called earlier.' Tears welled up in her eyes as she spoke. 'What if it's too late?'

Adrenalin coursed through me as I thought of the dog lying in the garden behind me, dead.

The woman's husband walked round the van and put his arm around her. 'It'll be all right, you'll see.' He didn't sound very convincing.

Tony opened the back door of the van and pulled out the two graspers. He kept hold of the brand new one, and handed me the older one, which had many teeth marks all over the thick, plastic tubing that coated the wire.

'I'm going to open the gate slightly, and try and slip this over the dog's head. If you push yours through underneath mine, you may be able to loop it over while it's watching me. Either way, if one of us can get hold of it, I'll take the grasper and you can go in.' He looked at me, with such a serious expression on his face. 'Okay?'

I nodded, but didn't speak.

'Right – let's go,' he said.

As soon as we neared the back gate, the dog lunged at it, and my heart missed a few beats. *What if it gets out? What if it attacks Tony? What am I going to do?* For the first time in my life I was scared of a dog.

Tony tried to hold the gate tight against the metal pole with his left hand, while at the same time trying to push the grasper through the slight opening with his right hand, but, unable to manoeuvre it properly, he couldn't get near the dog. I tried to get the noose over its head while it watched what Tony was doing, but it felt the wire touch its neck and pulled back. Leaping once more at the gate, it landed both front paws close to Tony's hand, crushing it between the gate and post. His face screwed up in pain as he pulled his hand out, but one look over the fence at the prostrate body of the other dog made him grab the gate again and keep trying.

Once, he nearly got her, but just as he tightened the noose around her neck, she jerked backwards and the wire slipped over her left ear and off. We both groaned audibly. By then, my back was aching like mad from being bent over in such an awkward position, so I stood upright and stretched.

'Time is not on our side, and this isn't working,' Tony said to the couple, who had watched in total silence. 'What's the dog normally like?'

The husband answered, 'She's a bit nervous, and she does seem to prefer women to men.'

His wife added, 'I often feed them over the fence and they're both very friendly then.'

'Do you have anything you could coax her with, just to get her away from the gate so that we can gain access?' asked Tony.

'I've got some biscuits; she loves biscuits,' the woman responded. 'I'll go straight in and call her over.'

Tony looked grim. Although he realised by now that the dog was unlikely to move, he couldn't help keep glancing over the fence, just in case. 'If we don't get to it soon, it may well be too late – that's if it isn't too late already.'

'Come on then … come on then …' The woman was standing on something and leaning right over the six foot, panel fence that joined the two gardens, waving a biscuit at the dog. In an instant, the dog's attitude changed, and wagging her tail she trotted over to the woman. 'Come on then … there's a good girl …' The woman continued to ply the dog with bits of biscuit.

Tony pushed the gate open and walked along the edge of the garden towards the prone dog, trying to be as quiet as possible, but the bitch caught sight of him and, growling, turned from the biscuits towards him. My heart leapt into my mouth as I opened the gate wider, ready to go in with my grasper, totally aware of how futile my effort would be.

'COME ON THEN ... COME ON THEN ... THERE'S A GOOD GIRL,' the woman shrieked. The dog stopped momentarily, with her head down and lips curled. She stared at Tony and snarled, before turning back for more biscuits.

I felt a trickle of sweat run down the side of my face as Tony crouched down, and gently pushed his arms underneath the prone dog. As he lifted the body from the ground, the dog's head hung over the side of his arm, mouth agape, tongue dangling. As he walked back towards the gate, its legs and tail swung, knocking against his knees lifelessly, with each step he took. I put both my hands to my mouth as I gasped.

I looked across at the woman, and her crumpled face said it all – but somehow she kept the dog's attention, and carried on feeding her the biscuits.

I came to my senses when Tony got to the gate, and I helped him ease the dog through before closing it behind him. He laid the dog on the ground, and opened its right eye. There was no reaction. We stared at it in silence, and it felt like an age had gone by before we saw its ribcage expand – ever so slightly. We both heaved sighs of relief and sprang into action.

At the same time as he asked me to open up the back of the van, I was opening up the back of the van. I grabbed a folded blanket and quickly shook it out, then helped Tony position the dog's head so that it could breathe as easily as possible. The dog felt cold – really cold, even though it had been lying in the hot sun, so we covered it in more blankets after adjusting its legs so that it at least looked comfortable. Simultaneously, we opened the side doors and got in.

Tony started his engine as the woman reappeared, wringing her hands with distress. She whispered, 'Is he gone?'

Tony took his foot off the accelerator. 'No, he's breathing, but only just. I'll be in touch.' I smiled at her, but she didn't see it because we'd gone.

At the veterinary surgery, the locum vet took one look at the dog. 'Jesus …' he said quietly.

Within seconds, rehydration fluid was being intravenously dripped into the dog via his right foreleg, and as the vet bandaged the needle in place, he yelled his orders with urgency. A veterinary nurse drew up various liquids and passed them to the vet who injected them into the dog's rump, while another nurse took the dog's temperature, which, as we already knew, was far too low.

I stood there feeling utterly useless, and as I stroked his cold ears, random sentences between the vet and his assistants punctured my thoughts. 'His pulse is very weak.' 'There isn't an ounce of fat in his entire body.' 'His gums are colourless.' 'I'd like to kill the bastard that did this to him …'

Finally, the nurses carried him to a metal cage which had already been prepared, including a large heat pad underneath the thick fleecy bedding. I knelt next to him, continuing to stroke his ears through the wire, and listened as the vet told Tony that it was the worst cruelty case he'd ever seen. I looked at the dog's head; big, broad, handsome – then at his wasted body. Then I cried.

Tony gave me his hanky. 'Come on, wipe the tears away, we've got a dog to catch.'

'What?' I sniffed.

'We have to go back and collect the other Shepherd cross. The owners haven't been seen for some days, so we can't leave her there. Come on.'

'Oh, for God's sake,' I grumbled, as I blew my nose, 'here we go again.' But I'd been hoping we would be going back for her.

Unexpectedly, she allowed Tony to put the noose around her neck without a murmur, and even wagged her tail as she jumped into the back of his van. He put a check chain and lead on her, and pulled the trigger to release the grasper. There was no need for it after all.

Personalized printed cards were issued to all RSPCA Inspectors, giving the national number of the RSPCA, and the name and number of the Inspector who had called. Before we left, Tony leaned on the roof of the van and added his own message asking the owners to contact him urgently, before putting it through the letter box.

Back at the animal centre the bitch, who was a bit lean, but not thin, wolfed down a small bowl of cereal-based dog food before being led into her kennel. She drank for ages, almost emptying the bowl, then stood, with her front paws resting against the wire door, wagging her tail furiously.

The next morning I listened when Tony rang the vet. 'Hello there. It's Tony from the RSPCA. I just wondered how the German Shepherd cross was? He's regained conscious-ness? Good. Good.' He gave me the thumbs up sign.

I stood up and went to stand in front of the fireplace, and thanked God as I wiped away my tears.

Six days later, Tony opened up the back of his van, and lying there, weak but definitely alive, was the emaciated dog.

I got the bitch out of the kennel and took her to the van, and I'm quite sure it wasn't just my eyes that misted over when she jumped straight into the back, whined quietly, then gently licked the other dog's face all over.

In the kennel, she mothered him, licking not just his eyes and ears, but all of him, even between his toes, and that night she lay next to him on the blanket, rather than in the plastic bed she had been sleeping in. It reminded me of Titan and Sophie, and I wondered for probably the millionth time how people could be so cruel.

When Anna took the bitch out for a walk the next morning, it was the saddest thing to watch the dog's feeble attempt to get up and follow, and then to have to listen to his quiet whine because she wasn't there.

It was another two days before Tony met the owners. 'The dogs are called Rocky and Mandy. They're only about eighteen months old, and the owners have had them since they were six weeks. They're brother and sister, and neither of them is neutered yet.'

'So what excuses have they given you for the state of him?' I asked.

'The man said he's never eaten much, and that he always left most of the food they gave him. I said that was very strange as he'd eaten everything put in front of him and had already put on over a pound in weight while he had been at the veterinary surgery, which was for just under a week.'

'Nice one.' I smiled. 'Did they say why Rocky was shut out all the time, and Mandy wasn't?'

'Yes, though they both gave different answers. He said Rocky liked living outside. She said the dog cocked his leg up everything indoors so he wasn't allowed in.'

'I'll go with what she said then,' I replied. 'It doesn't make sense though, does it? They obviously fed Mandy, but not Rocky. How could someone feed one dog, but not the other?'

'I doubt we'll ever know the true reason,' Tony replied, 'but my thoughts are that they just couldn't be bothered. For a start, they admitted they'd been away for several days and hadn't arranged for anyone to care for the dogs during their absence. The wife said she never fed the dogs as it was her husband who'd wanted them, not her, and her husband said that he worked all hours and didn't get home till late every evening and he thought his wife had fed them.'

'How stupid to contradict each other like that. Did they get angry with each other?' I asked.

'I interviewed them separately. Neither of them knew what the other had said in their statements, though I expect they've discussed it since and will both realise that they've said different things.'

'Oh dear, that's going to cause problems between them then.' I imagined the argument that most likely followed Tony's visit. 'I suppose we now have the same long wait that we had with Titan and Sophie; we won't know if they're going to get the dogs back until the case – that's if there is a case – is heard.'

'No. They've signed the dogs over already. They seemed quite relieved to, actually. The wife said there was no way she was prepared to keep them after all this anyway.'

'Great! So we don't have to worry about that then! Anna will be chuffed too. It's the worst thing – not knowing if they have to go back to the very people that caused them to suffer in the first place.' I gritted my teeth. 'No animal should EVER have to go back.'

'Unfortunately, it's not for us to decide, but I do agree with you.' He added, 'I've advised them to speak to a solicitor, and said that I'm sending a report to HQ for their perusal. The vet has already given me a statement, saying that in his opinion the dog has been caused unnecessary suffering. He's been very thorough, and given plenty of detail about the condition the dog was in when he first had contact with it. He's also said he believed the dog would undoubtedly have died that day had it not received treatment.'

I thought about how lucky Rocky actually was; if the neighbours hadn't cared … if they hadn't called when they did … the dog would now be dead. And after all the suffering he'd gone through, no-one would have known anything about it – except, of course, his owners. I whispered, 'Oh God, that poor dog. It was so close.'

'Yes, it was far too close. I'll bring out some record sheets for you and Anna to fill in; what he eats, his weight gain, vet visits and so on. I'm hoping that we can prosecute the pair of them for abandoning both dogs, as well as for causing unnecessary suffering to Rocky.'

'Oh. Can you be accused of abandoning a pet if you leave it at home like that?' I asked. 'I thought that to abandon an animal, you had to take it outside and literally throw it out.'

'No. If you don't make any provision for an animal to be cared for while you're away, technically, you have abandoned that animal, even if it's in your own home.'

'Well, I hope HQ let you take proceedings against them for everything you can, they damn well deserve it.'

Anna poked her head round the office door. 'Just to let you know that the Shepherd cross is up, and having a wobbly wander on the grass. I've put the bitch in the top run with my lot for a while so she can't knock him over.'

'We know their names now: Rocky and Mandy,' Tony said, as we followed Anna outside.

Tony stood, with his hands on his hips and smiled. 'Well, well. He's making good progress.' He walked over to Rocky and stroked his head, telling him what a lucky boy he was at the same time.

'Well, Rocky, it's a good job I'm not a magistrate,' Anna told him, 'I'd have your owners hung, drawn and quartered; in fact, I wouldn't have it done, I'd do it myself – and enjoy it.'

'Sounds good to me. I'd come and watch, or help if you wanted,' I chipped in.

Anna laughed now. 'Oooh no. I wouldn't want any help. It'd take away some of my pleasure.'

'I think I shall leave you ladies to your gory conversation. See you later.' Tony blew me a kiss as he made his way to the van.

It was two more weeks before Rocky was able to walk properly, but when he did, it was a pleasure to see the joy he had for life. Everything fascinated him: a Red Admiral butterfly which landed on a flower in front of him; ears of corn rustling against each other as they blew in the wind; my cats, which he watched with pricked-up ears and head tilted sideways, before trying to take their heads gently into his mouth. His tail never stopped wagging, even when he was having a wee, and when he was lying on his blanket, snoozing, the very tip of it would thump up and down when someone walked past. Even after everything he'd been through, he was still the most loving, affectionate dog you could wish for.

'The good news is HQ are going for abandonment of both dogs, as well as causing unnecessary suffering to Rocky,' Tony said as he walked in through the office door.

'Will that be both of them, or just the husband?' I asked.

'Both of them,' he replied.

'Does that mean I can't tar and feather them now?' asked Anna.

'You want to tar and feather, as well as hang, draw and quarter them?' Tony laughed.

'Of course, they deserve it. No getting off lightly with me.'

'I agree with you – absolutely,' he replied, 'but I think a stiff fine, costs awarded to the RSPCA, and a ban on keeping dogs would be sufficient. The thought of a prison sentence is rather appealing, but unlikely.'

Anna thought for a moment. 'Hmm, as long as they do have to pay all of the costs, and get a whacking great fine – say, ten thousand, and are banned for life from keeping dogs, I might agree with that.'

I giggled. 'You'd be a brilliant magistrate; teach the others a thing or two about how to hand out a proper sentence.'

'Oh I'd hand a proper sentence out all right. I'd leap over the magistrate's bench in my RSPCA dungarees, brandishing my pot of tar and a duck feather pillow.'

As I answered the phone, I couldn't help smiling at the image that Anna had just conjured up for me.

Rocky adored everyone, even the vet, who was always given a slobbery welcome, but he saved his most rapturous greetings for a particular young girl. She visited weekly, and spent most of her time in one of the outside grass runs, playing with him and Mandy. Her name was Vicky, and she was about seventeen years old. We knew little about her, except that her father dropped her off, and then an hour or so later, picked her up – and that she was very shy.

Over the weeks I watched as the bond between her and Rocky grew stronger, but I was still surprised when one Saturday, she asked if she could take him and Mandy out for a walk. I thought they would be too strong for her and expressed my concern, but said she could try walking them around the animal centre first to see how it went.

They both pulled, eager to get out, but Vicky was stronger than she looked, and reined them both in with a sharp 'Heel.' Although they didn't understand what 'heel' meant, they did understand what the tug on the leads meant, and both stopped and waited. With a big smile, I motioned to her to take them out through the gate, waved and shouted, 'Have fun!' then watched as she trotted them off down to the field.

'Hello,' said Vicky's father.

'Hello. Vicky's walking dogs in the field next door. Do you want me to go and find her?'

'Oh no … no. I'll wait, thank you. Has she got Rocky and Mandy with her by any chance?'

'Yes she has. I was a bit worried about whether she'd cope with both of them, but she got them under control straight away.'

Her father smiled. 'She keeps on about them all the time. We lost our old German Shepherd a few months ago. Vicky grew up with him, and loved doing obedience training with him. They were very close, right to the end. She was devastated.'

'Oh, I bet she was. I know that feeling too.' I immediately got an image of Scamper, my Doberman cross, who had to be put to sleep just before I moved to the animal centre. For a second, I was deep in thought.

I shook my head clear. 'So – she's into obedience then? I thought she handled them well. Are you looking for another dog?'

'Not actively. Not here anyway. We live in London and come here to visit relatives, but since Vicky was brought to the centre by one of her cousins, we can't keep her away.' He smiled. 'I've told her not to get attached to any of the dogs; I know all animal centres have their own boundaries, and I know we are well outside yours.'

'Well, boundary rules were made to be broken – under certain circumstances.' I laughed. 'So if you are looking for a dog – or maybe I should say two dogs, let me know, and I can arrange for another animal centre to carry out a home-check. We do re-home out of our area if we believe it's in the best interests of the animal. Anyway, I don't want to push you either way, but have a think about it.'

'Thank you; thank you very much. I'll talk to my wife this evening. Ah, there's Vicky.' He walked towards his daughter, who had the biggest smile on her face.

The day of the court case arrived, and for the first time, I was accompanying Tony.

'Are you ready?' he asked as we stood on the steps leading up to the courthouse.

I took a deep breath. 'Yes. As ready as I'll ever be for something like this.' I felt sick, and regretted my decision to go because I had no idea how I was going to react when I came face to face with the people who had caused Rocky so much hurt. Knowing how I felt, Tony linked his arm through mine, squeezed tightly, and led me through the courthouse doors.

Inside, we were greeted by a gentleman in long black robes, who shook our hands vigorously before disappearing off behind two heavy wooden doors. The RSPCA solicitor arrived just after us, and took Tony to one side for several minutes.

'Is everything okay?' I whispered.

'Yes, it's fine. You don't need to whisper,' he whispered back.

I elbowed him in the ribs, but smiled, and felt a bit less anxious.

An RSPCA Chief Inspector appeared, along with two more Inspectors, all dressed like Tony in their Number 1 uniforms. I saw the shiny toe caps on the shoes of the other three, and thought back to when I'd laughed at Tony for spending stupid amounts of time doing 'spit and polish' on his. Now I understood, and suddenly realised how proud I felt to be standing with them, to be a part of the society we all worked for. Sadly, I realised just how much they were all at home in the surroundings.

I recognised a journalist from the local paper, who was talking among a group of men and women, all carrying note pads. Two of them also had camera bags slung over their shoulders. I hoped they were waiting for our cruelty case.

The case was to be one of the first heard, but Tony had warned me that there could be a long wait, and said that it was likely to be adjourned as the owners had pleaded not guilty. He was right. Four hours had gone by in the waiting room, copious plastic cups of coffee had been drunk, hasty visits to the toilet had been made, and the case was apparently no closer to being heard. I was dying for a cigarette, and looking at Tony, knew he would be too.

Then it was lunch time. With relief, we went outside and I inhaled my cigarette smoke as deeply as I could.

The afternoon followed the same pattern, until the RSPCA solicitor came over, with a big beam on his face. 'They've just accepted their solicitor's advice – at last – and have changed their plea to guilty. We are in courtroom two shortly. I'll read all the statements out and the magistrates will decide on the sentence.'

Tony looked straight at me. 'Happy?'

I was stunned by the news, and hadn't properly taken it in, but responded, 'Yes; I think so. Does that mean they won't get such big sentences?'

'No. It doesn't make any difference. The magistrates will listen to all the statements and make their decisions based on those, not on whether the owners have pleaded guilty. What it does mean is that we'll know their decision today, so no more waiting – and the dogs can go to their new home.'

I wanted to cry, as usual, but bit my lip instead.

A home-check had already been done, and Vicky's parents were adopting both Rocky and Mandy. Needless to say, Vicky was ecstatic, and had been waiting anxiously for this day to arrive.

As we continued to wait, I imagined the two dogs walking with Vicky, playing with Vicky, doing obedience with Vicky, and from what her father had said, sleeping on Vicky's bed, just like her old Shepherd had.

The usher appeared, and led us into courtroom number two, where we all sat to the left of the magistrate's bench.

'Are they journalists?' I whispered to Tony, as five men and women, still clutching note pads, were shown to a row of seats opposite us.

He nodded. 'They've been waiting all day for this case. Matthew from the local paper spoke to me earlier and said there'd been a lot of interest from the national papers. No-one likes cruelty to animals.'

A large woman in a bright red cardigan, carrying a plastic flowery shopping bag, sat herself down on the end seat opposite the bench. She got out a packet of wine gums and started sucking one. A young lad, in jeans and T-shirt jumped over her and sat half way along the row. She leaned over and asked him if he wanted a wine gum. He took one and winked at her.

'Who are they?' I asked Tony, quietly.

'Just curious members of the public, I expect. Anyone is allowed to sit in on a case, if they want to.'

'Oh. I didn't realise. Think I might do it myself later, but I'll pass on any future cruelty cases though.'

A youngish couple arrived, preceded by a large gentleman in a pinstriped suit who was carrying a bunch of papers under his arm and a briefcase in his hand. He showed them to seats near the bench, separate from the rest of us, before sitting at another bench, in the middle of the courtroom.

She wore a skirt suit in pale green, and her face was caked in foundation. He was quite scruffy, with a white, open necked shirt, which had a stain on the front, and casual trousers with frayed hems. He walked in with his hands in his pockets.

Tony nudged me and turned his head in their direction. It was them.

My pulse quickened, my mouth went dry and my breathing became rapid. I trembled as I filled my eyes – my face – with pure hatred as I glared at them.

'ALL RISE.'

As Tony put his hand under my arm to make me stand, I pulled my eyes away from them and watched as the three magistrates walked into the courtroom and took their seats.

It was strange sitting there listening to the RSPCA solicitor read all the statements out, especially when he got to mine; it didn't feel as if it was me that had written it. And by the time he'd finished reading out the one made by the vet, I realised that I wasn't the only one crying; a woman reporter and the lady in the red cardigan were also wiping their eyes. At least I'd come prepared, with a pocket full of loo roll; the reporter was using her sleeve.

'THE MAGISTRATES WILL NOW RETIRE. ALL RISE.'

We headed straight for the door, and had the cigarettes out before we reached the bottom step. I managed to smoke two in the short time that we had before going back for the verdict.

'ALL RISE.'

This was it. This was what I'd been waiting for. Justice, for Rocky and Mandy. Everybody sat down, except the couple, who had been told to remain standing.

The magistrate shuffled the paper in front of him before looking at them, for the first time. 'You have both pleaded guilty …'

She started to cry.

I stared at her. *Cry, you bitch. Go on …*

The magistrate continued, 'You will pay a fine of …'

I clenched my hands tight as the tears rolled down my cheeks. *Ban them – please, ban them …*

'You will pay all costs to the RSPCA, the total amount being …'

She crumbled down onto the seat, sobbing. He looked as white as his shirt, but continued to stand.

There was a slight pause.

Oh God – come on, please …

'You will be banned from keeping dogs for …'

I wanted to jump up and down and punch the air and shout and scream, but I quietly followed Tony.

As we left, journalists and camera men surrounded the group of RSPCA Inspectors, asking for any comments on their opinions of the sentencing. I wasn't interested in any of that, so took myself off to the edge of the steps where I sat down, and took a deep breath.

It was done. The dogs could go home.

Anna grabbed my arm as we walked down to the gate. 'I love it when they go, but I hate it too.'

'I know exactly what you mean.' We stopped, and watched as Vicky's dad closed the car door on Vicky, Rocky and Mandy. I sniffed.

'They will be happy there.' Anna tugged me, then she sniffed too.

'I know; very happy. And they've promised to come and visit us.' I ran the back of my hand over my eyes as the car engine started.

'BYE!' Anna shouted, waving frantically.

'SEE YOU SOON.' I added, in a choked voice.

Vicky hung out of the window. 'THANK YOU SO MUCH.'

As they disappeared round the corner, we stood and looked at each other and, through the tears, laughed.

'Come on, you silly old cow,' said Anna, 'let's go and have a cuppa before we start the feeds.'

CHAPTER 12

For the Love of Bertie

As Bertie sat on top of the open living room window, waiting for Tony to come home, I thought for the umpteenth time that she needed a friend – a parrot-type friend. She had behaved reasonably well over the last few months, apart from picking huge holes in the curtains, shrieking incessantly when the phone rang or the dogs fought, and wandering around the cottage attacking anything that happened to be in her path but I felt that she was a bit lonely sometimes.

'There's a parrot for sale in the local pet shop,' I said to Tony that evening.

He lowered his newspaper and stared at me for several seconds. 'You're obviously telling me that for a reason.'

'Bertie gets lonely when you're out, and I think she needs some company.'

'Bertie has plenty of company – the house is never empty.' He adjusted his newspaper and carried on reading.

Stubbornly, I continued. 'She needs PARROT company, not human, dog or cat. I don't like having only one of something – look at Lucy the sheep; she was so much happier when she went to live with the other sheep.'

The newspaper went down onto the table with just a tiny bit of force. 'Janie, darling. I don't think Bertie has ever seen another parrot, so she wouldn't even know that she is a parrot, therefore, I doubt very much that she is in need of the company of another parrot.' He shook his head as he returned to his newspaper.

'He's an African Grey. One of his wings has been broken, probably when he was captured, and it sticks out at an angle. The owner of the shop said no-one wants him because of it, and told me I could have him for two hundred and fifty pounds.'

I heard the choked sort of snort Tony made before he carefully folded the newspaper and placed it flat on the table. He smoothed the crease with the palm of his hand as he leaned towards me. 'That is a ridiculous amount of money. Darling, it's been months since Tina ate the sofa, and I've only recently been able to order a new suite; we cannot afford to pay two hundred and fifty pounds for a parrot to keep Bertie company.'

'I know it's a lot of money, but apparently they cost about four hundred pounds these days, so it's a really good price.'

Tony inhaled deeply as he stood up and walked towards the door, where he stopped, turned and faced me. 'Bertie is not lonely. She does not need another parrot to keep her company, and we do not have that sort of money to spend on anything. And that … is my final word.'

We called the new parrot Percyphone.

Tony was very pleased with the price of the huge cage he was trying to fit into the back of his van. 'Just shows how much profit they make on goods if they can let them go for half price.'

I smiled at his unexpected enthusiasm. 'I wouldn't dream of haggling the way you do. I'd have paid the full price for it, so I'm really glad you came with me.' I was also really glad that he'd given in and allowed me to get the parrot, and couldn't wait to get home to Bertie and introduce them to each other.

Bertie was extremely interested in the new cage, and helped Tony by holding the plastic food and water bowls in her beak for him. She examined it thoroughly, inside and out, and gave her approval to the perch that sat on the opened up top by carrying a piece of nectarine up to it for a snack.

With the cage installed next to Bertie's stand, and Bertie perched on Tony's chest with another slice of nectarine, I took the cardboard carrier containing Percyphone into the living room and opened it up. The four-year-old African Grey quietly climbed out, and after a furtive look around, went straight to the food bowl and took a piece of apple to munch.

I looked at Bertie, who had stiffened as soon as she saw the bird, and smiled. 'Look Bertie, a new friend for you.' Without further ado, Bertie made her way to the cage and climbed up the wire.

'TONY. TONY. TONY,' she shrieked at the top of her voice, as she lunged through the bars and grabbed viciously at the broken wing of the parrot.

'Hey! You evil little cow!' I shouted at her, astonished at her outburst.

'Bertie, pack it in.' Tony put his arm out to her as he spoke. She climbed up to his neck, grumbling quietly to him as she went, before burying her head under his jumper.

I was crestfallen.

'It'll work out all right. She'll soon get used to him,' Tony said in a positive voice.

'Yes. Of course she will,' I responded, uncertainly. 'I should have expected that really, knowing what she's like.'

The next morning I woke with a good feeling; the parrots were going to get along fine.

'BERTIE, STOP IT,' yelled Kelley.

Oh that bloody bird ... now what ... I put the kettle down and went into the living room to find Bertie already climbing back up to her perch.

'What did she do?'

'She walked along the back of Shanie's chair and tried to pull her hair out,' replied Kelley.

'But I'm okay; she didn't get me,' added Shanie.

'Oh Bertie, you really are horrible.' My glare was lost on her as she cracked open a walnut.

Before I'd finished making the girls their cups of tea, Kelley shrieked again. 'BERTIE. NO. DON'T DO THAT.'

'Now what?' Bertie was sitting on top of Percyphone's cage, scraping her beak backwards and forwards along the bars.

'Mummy ... Bertie just tried to pull the wallpaper off,' said Shanie.

'What! Where?'

Shanie pointed to the wall next to where Bertie was sitting, still rubbing her beak along the wire and looking for all the world like she was sharpening it. There, just at the join, was a small piece of paper that had been pulled away from the wall.

'Oh Bertie; don't start doing that,' I huffed at her. 'Lisa, can you take her back to her stand for me, love?' Lisa was still the only one who could handle the bird when Tony was out.

The girls had gone off on the school bus, and I was getting Edwina ready to go to play school, when April and Tina had one of their nearly fights. This always sent Bertie into fits of screeching and wing flapping, and in full flow, she slid down the metal pole of the stand to go and attack whichever dog she came across first. My deaf, twelve-year-old Basset cross, Tuppy, appeared to be her target this time, so as I screamed at the dogs to stop it, I scooped her up before Bertie reached her, and having plonked her on the armchair out of the way, set about grabbing April and Tina.

Bent over and out of breath with the struggle of pulling them apart, I held onto each snarling dog by the scruff of its neck, then realised that Edwina was giggling in the doorway. Following her gaze, I let out a shriek – Bertie had Percyphone by the tail, and was pulling it for all she was worth. Poor Percyphone was leaning as far forward on his perch as he could, trying to pull away from her.

'BERTIE!' Just as I got to her, she released his tail feathers, and he catapulted upside down. With his feet still clutching his perch, he stopped only when he managed to hook his beak into the wire.

Furious I went towards Bertie, but she was off, back to her stand, squawking and lunging at the dogs as she went.

I sat down on the nearest chair, exhausted.

'Bertie is very naughty, isn't she, Mummy?' my young daughter said.

'Yes love, to us, she is being very naughty, but really she's just being a parrot.' I heaved a huge sigh.

We eventually left for play school, and were only a little bit late.

Bertie shared Tony's chips that evening, followed by a bowl of her very favourite human food, cornflakes, with milk but no sugar, and she behaved herself until Tony went into the kitchen to make coffee.

'Bertie,' Tony snapped, waking me up from my doze.

'What's she up to now,' I asked as I stretched.

'Pulling the wallpaper off.' He put her back onto her stand.

'Oh, not again.' I sat up and looked at where Bertie had been sitting, and there was a good sized patch of bare wall, with a pile of shredded paper on the floor beneath.

'It's my fault, isn't it?' I said to Tony. 'It's because of Percyphone. She never did this before.' For the first time, I regretted getting the new parrot.

'No, she didn't pull the wallpaper off, but she did make holes in the curtains. I'm sure in time she will get used to him, and who knows – may even get to like him.' Tony smiled at me. 'Coffee?'

'Hmm, I like your optimism, and I thank you for it, but I don't share it; not any more. You know as well as I do that she doesn't like Percyphone, and I doubt anything is going to change that. And yes please to the coffee.' I sat back and watched Bertie, who was now swaying in time to the theme tune of *Minder*.

Next morning Marie was working, and she poked her head round the back door. 'Oh shit. Oh shit. Oh shit,' she said to Bertie, who was sitting on Tony's shoulder, holding the spoon ready for their breakfast. 'Morning Tony,' she added.

Bertie carefully transferred the spoon from her beak to her foot. 'MORNING. MORNING. PRETTY BOY. MORNING.' She bobbed her head up and down as she shrieked back at Marie, drowning out Tony's response.

Marie grinned. She had successfully taught Bertie to say 'morning' but had had no luck getting her to swear. She gave Bertie half a plum. 'There's a man with a three-piece suite out here.' She called as she went.

The girls rushed out, and in their excitement, got in everyone's way as the first chair was carried into the living room.

'Oh come on you lot, get out of the way!' I said as I pulled Edwina to the side to avoid her getting wedged in the doorway with the sofa. As they helped Tony pull off the cellophane wrapping, I ran my hand along the top of one of the chairs, admiring the grain of the oak frame; the quality of the detail in the carving.

'Oh wow. This is really lovely, Tony.' He'd chosen it on his own, and ordered it as a surprise, so this was the first time I'd seen it. I flopped down onto one of the antique red leather chairs. 'Thank you so much, I love it.' I grinned at him. 'Only one problem; your old recliner.'

'My old recliner … is not … a problem,' he responded.

I laughed. We'd argued about his old recliner many times. It was like an ancient teddy bear, threadbare arms and foot rest, buttons missing, and tufts of innards hanging out in various places. The only difference was that ancient teddies looked well loved – his recliner just looked tatty.

'But it is a problem. There's no room for it, and it looks even worse now.' I stroked the leather arm of the new sofa, and teased, 'Like an old nag among thoroughbreds.'

He stopped cutting the cellophane wrapping, leaned on the back of the sofa and tried to give me a warning look. 'My dear old recliner is the most comfortable chair I've ever had. It fits me perfectly. It stays.'

I laughed at him. 'Ooo, getting all defensive, eh? Okay! The recliner stays.' I continued in a more serious tone, 'I think now would be a good time to move Percyphone's cage, though. Bertie would probably be a lot happier if he wasn't in here; the dining room would be a good place. What do you think?'

'Yes, I think that would be better for both of them. His cage will probably just fit in next to the table, and he'd be able to see out of the window as well. Let's move him now. It may even mean there's enough room for my old nag …'

Bertie loved not having Percyphone in the living room, and was quite amenable for a couple of days. She only pulled Tina's tail once, as she wandered across the floor to retrieve a hazelnut that she'd dropped, and she only tried to pull my hair out once, while I was engrossed in reading the newspaper. Fortunately, Lisa walked into the living room at that moment and got to her just as she was about to strike.

But the peace didn't last. She found Percyphone.

Percyphone was a lovely parrot. He took everything in his stride, and ignored the daily, murderous attempts that Bertie now made on him. He savoured his pieces of fruit and happily emitted exotic-sounding whoops and whistles. His favourite thing was to have a mist of water sprayed over his entire body, when he would stretch out his wings to get the full benefit of the shower, and then spend an age preening himself. He was the antithesis of Bertie.

'SHUTUPSHUTUPSHUTUP ...' Bertie's latest thing was to yell at the dogs when they barked at the door bell. My Mum always told them to shut up when they started, but, unlike Bertie, she sort of whispered it.

'Oh great; Bertie has added to her repertoire,' I groaned to Tony. 'Why couldn't it be something nice, like "I love Percyphone"?'

And since she'd had to spend a lot more of her time wandering across the floor in order to carry out her daily assaults on Percyphone, she'd also become more antagonistic towards the dogs. She often pulled a tail, or tweaked an ear, when the dogs were fast asleep. They watched her constantly now, and leapt up onto the furniture if she went anywhere near them. Sometimes April even stopped barking at the door to look around, presumably to see if Bertie was behind her.

Strangely, Tuppy wasn't intimidated at all, and if Bertie went near her, she bared her toothless gums and snapped at the bird. For some reason it worked, and Bertie tended to leave her alone, most of the time.

I had to admit to Tony that over the last few weeks, one good thing had come out of the parrot situation – but only one. Tina and April hadn't had a nearly fight for quite some time.

'TONY. TONY. TONY.'

'Where is she?' I asked him, as we unloaded the shopping from the back of the van. She sounded quite distant.

'I really can't tell. But she's certainly not on the living room window.' He craned his neck and listened, his gaze finally coming to rest on the weeping willow that graced the farthest corner of our huge front garden.

'Is that her?' He pointed towards the topmost branches of the tree.

I shaded my eyes from the sun and squinted at the tree, and saw a definite blue and yellow disturbance happening among the leaves. 'Oh my God. Yes; that's her!'

'BERTIE!' called Tony, frantically, as we hurried through the side gate into the garden.

She saw us, and screeched 'TONYTONYPRETTYBOY-TONY' just as frantically back at him.

I always found it hilarious when she called him pretty boy, and now was no exception; I giggled as we neared the bottom of the tree.

'This really isn't funny.' Tony had a hurt expression on his face. 'She's frightened, you can tell by the tone of her voice.'

'I'm sorry, it's just funny when she calls you pretty boy, that's all. I know she's scared, but the important thing is – what are we going to do now?' I stared at him, but he was pre-occupied. Bertie was trying to climb down, and doing a terrible job of it.

'She keeps going along the branches,' Tony muttered to himself, as he walked around to other side of the trunk to get a better view of her.

'Shall I go and get Marie?' I asked. 'I'm sure she would be able to climb up there and get her.'

'I'm sure you're right, Marie would be able to climb up the tree no problem, but it's risky; the branches are small and some of them may not take her weight. I don't want her to get hurt.'

I snorted at him. 'Marie wouldn't take any unnecessary risks and you know it. You also know how much she thinks of Bertie, and would want to get up there and at least try to help her down. I'm going to get her.' I stomped off to find Marie.

Marie looked up into the leafy branches, and whistled quietly. 'Oh shit. Oh shit. Oh shit. Literally,' she said. 'All right bird – I'm coming up. Don't move.'

She didn't need the ladder that Tony had rested against the trunk – but climbed up it anyway.

'Oh SHIT,' we heard after a couple of minutes, then watched the Homburg-style hat she always wore sail down and wedge on one of the lower branches.

'Marie; are you all right?' Tony called out. He sounded worried.

'Yeah. Lost my hat though,' she shouted back.

I couldn't help giggling again, much to Tony's consternation.

Various mutterings of 'Oh shit' wafted down to us over the minutes, and Tony asked Marie repeatedly if she was all right. I think she must have wanted to save him asking, because the next 'Oh shit' was tagged with 'Got a bloody branch stuck down the back of my T-shirt and nearly choked myself.'

The worst 'Oh shit' was the last one, and was accompanied by loud thuds as a huge branch crashed down through the leaves, hitting bough after bough on its way.

'OH MY GOD,' I yelled as loudly as I could. 'MAREEE …'

'OHSHITOHSHITOHSHITOHSHIT,' Bertie screamed.

The ground shuddered under our feet as the bough landed, and as if in slow motion, it rolled, gouging a large hole in the grass before coming to rest, just to the left of us. Hundreds of leaves floated down in its wake.

Tony and I looked at each other, stunned.

'Jesus. Bertie nearly went then,' Marie shouted. 'I shoved a rotten branch to get it out of the way, and it knocked her as it fell. I just managed to grab her.'

'Thank goodness,' Tony whispered.

I collapsed against him, and wiped away the tears of relief. I would never – ever, ask Marie to climb another tree – ever again.

Marie climbed down a lot quicker than she climbed up, and proudly presented Bertie to a very anxious Tony. 'There you go Tone. She had me worried for a moment there, I can tell you. When that branch bashed her, I thought she was a gonner.' She scratched Bertie under her beak.

'And we thought you were a gonner,' said Tony. 'Thank you for retrieving our wayward parrot.'

'Did you hear her though,' Marie continued, 'she said "Oh shit!" Good eh! Can't wait to tell Mum. Oh shit – where's my hat?'

'Up there.' I pointed into the tree.

'Oh shit – here we go again.' She leapt up onto the branch, grabbed her hat, and leapt down. 'Well ladies and gentleman, that was fun, but I do have some work to do, so I'll be off.'

'Thank you very much, Marie,' Tony called after as she ran through the gate. She turned around and doffed her hat to him.

We made our leisurely way back, with Bertie chewing Tony's earlobe most of the way.

That episode seemed to be a turning point for Bertie. She never got to like Percyphone, but did stop attacking him, the dogs and the cats. She also left the wallpaper alone. We had to move one of our new chairs away from her stand because she still tried to pull our hair out, but we could live with that.

The front door bell rang, and the dogs erupted into a frenzy of barking. Percyphone's whoops and whistles drifted round to us through the open, dining room window. Bertie, sitting on top of the living room window, flapping her wings and screaming; 'OHSHITOHSHITOHSHIT,' completed the cacophony.

The delivery man looked sideways around me at the mass of bodies, baying as they jumped up at the gap in the door, then towards Bertie. His expression was one of amazement.

He shouted over the noise, 'CAN YOU SIGN FOR THIS PLEASE, LOVE?'

I took the pen and wrote my signature.

'IS IT ALWAYS LIKE THIS?' he yelled.

I nodded. 'Yep, it's always like this.'

'BLIMEY.' He laughed. 'KEEP YOU BUSY, DO THEY?'

'Oh yes, they keep me very busy,' I said loudly, and smiled.

We waved to each other as he walked back along the path, and as I turned into the cottage, and the noise abated, I grinned to myself. *Yes, it's always like this; and I wouldn't have it any other way.*

CHAPTER 13

4 lb of Poo

A blast of freezing air followed Tony as he struggled into the office with a large cardboard box under his arm.

'Oooh, it's cold today,' said Anna, as he closed the door.

We had a small electric fire in the room, but with the door being constantly in use it was impossible to keep the heat in. Anna cupped her hands round her mug of tea to keep them warm.

Tony put the box onto the desk and slid it towards me.

'WHAT is that smell?' I looked at him. 'It's disgusting. Where have you been?' I wrinkled up my nose as I scraped my chair back, grabbed my tea and stood behind Anna's dogs, which were all piled on top of each other on a rug in front of the fire.

'It's not me. Have a look,' he replied, pointing to the box.

With the box open, the stench was even worse. I immediately thought of Samson, and my heart sank as I held my breath. I looked at Tony, with a quizzical expression on my face, as all I'd revealed was a pile of matted fur. I retched as I pulled at the door to let in some fresh air.

'What the hell did that fur come off of? It's gross.' I gulped in the fresh air. 'I'm taking it outside. Thanks for that Tony.' I moved back towards the box and pulled one of the flaps.

'No. Have a closer look.' He held the top of the box open. 'It hasn't come from an animal – it is an animal.'

Anna got up and together we looked into the box as he picked up the lump of matted fur.

A leg hung down.

Anna gasped. 'It's a rabbit.'

It wriggled, and another leg appeared out of the mess.

I was speechless.

Tony put it on the floor, where it received a cursory sniff from Brodie, one of Anna's cross-breeds. He wasn't impressed, and moved round to the other side of the dog pile. The rabbit didn't move.

'Bloody hell – you can't tell which is its head and which is its tail.' Anna was now on her knees, examining it more thoroughly.

I joined her, and gently pulled at what looked like an ear, but the long fur on it had matted into the fur on its back and it wouldn't move. I tried to feel along its spine, but it was impossible to feel anything through the thick clumps.

'You can't even tell what colour it's supposed to be. Has the vet seen it yet?' I asked Tony.

'Yes. He weighed it but said it was difficult to tell the condition because of the state it's in. He checked in its mouth and the teeth are good. He's pretty sure it's very thin, but until all the fur is removed, can't really say much more.'

'Well, that's a bit strange, isn't it?' I straightened my back and looked up at him. 'Is he giving you a statement? And what about prosecuting the owner?'

'I've spoken to HQ, and there won't be a case. The vet knows. The neighbours called the police last night because the man was shouting and throwing things around in his flat, and they thought he was attacking someone, but it turned out that he was the only person there.

'Apparently he's been in and out of psychiatric hospitals for years because he goes through phases of not taking his medication. I don't know any more than that, except he's in no fit state to be taken to court, and someone at the hospital has signed the rabbit over to us already.'

'Do the neighbours know anything about the rabbit?' I asked.

'They didn't even know there was a rabbit in the flat as pets aren't allowed. It was just lucky that the man was in the bedroom when the police broke in, and one of the officers that attended noticed the awful smell coming from the wardrobe, and went to have a look.'

'Oh God – shut in a wardrobe for who knows how long … months, judging by the state of it.' I felt the prick of the tears as I picked up the stinking rabbit and turned it upside down. Urine dripped from its faeces-covered fur, and two little back legs dangled from the mess. A small nose was just visible, and it twitched when I stroked it. I looked at Anna, and almost gagging, said, 'Oh my God, where do we start?'

We took it in turns to clip the rabbit's fur, a bit at a time so as not to distress it, but it relished the attention that it received so much that I doubted anything would upset it.

'It's a boy!' said Anna a day later, as I walked past with several bowls full of dog food.

'Eh?'

'It's a boy. The tatty rabbit. I've just got to its nether region and found a testicle. Bless his little heart, his legs did shake a bit when I was snipping away down there, but he didn't move. Still got to find the other one though. See you later.' She disappeared back into the office.

After many hours clipping, over several days, we ended up with a very skinny, pedigree Angora.

'He's looking much better,' said Tony when the last of the matted fur was cut off his tail.

'Look at this.' I got the carrier bag in which we'd kept all the fur that we'd cut off, and put it on a set of scales. It went just over the four pound mark. 'That's how heavy all the shit was that he had to carry around with him, and he still doesn't weigh near half that himself.'

Tony whistled. 'It's pretty amazing that he was alive really. Apparently there was no food or water, and the wardrobe floor was sodden.'

I smiled at the rabbit. 'He is pretty amazing. Such character, bless him. He just sat there, throughout all the clipping and snipping. He loves the girls, and Anna's dogs too. He's feeling the cold now though, which is a bit of a worry. When I unlocked this morning he was shivering really badly. We've given him a massive amount of hay to nestle into, but after losing all that fur, I suppose he's bound to feel it.'

'Make him a coat.'

I looked at Tony. 'Pardon?'

'I said, make him a coat.'

I sighed. 'I heard what you said, but … he's a rabbit. You can't put a coat on a rabbit.'

'Why not?' Tony raised his eyebrows.

'I don't know, you just can't.' I looked at the rabbit and thought. My mum was good at knitting, and was always making jumpers for the girls, and little outfits for their dolls.

'Okay. I can't make him a coat, but I expect my mum can. I'll ask her.'

She was busy knitting when I went indoors – a red cardigan to go with the red trousers and bonnet she'd already finished. They were to clothe a new doll for Shanie, and were red because Christmas was just a few weeks away.

She laughed heartily at my request, but agreed to try, and said as long as red was okay she'd start it right now. I imagined the rabbit in a coat, and felt that it would look daft no matter what the colour, so told her red was fine.

I'd often envied my mum's ability to look at something and make an outfit for it – just like that – and today, I did so again. Within just a few hours of asking her, she presented me with a perfectly shaped rabbit coat, two layers thick.

The rabbit sat without moving as I carefully pushed the entire coat over his head. It was shaped to fit around his neck, and along his back, with a small, belt-type bit to go under his belly to keep it in place. The neck fitted him well, so I pulled his front legs through the hole and the belt bit wrapped nicely around his belly. The back covered him, right down to his bottom, but hung over his hind legs just a tiny bit too much, and when he hopped around the office floor he reminded me of Dopey from *Snow White*.

'Look at him!' said Anna, when she saw him the next day. 'Father Christmas, eat your heart out!'

'Not bad, eh?' I laughed. 'And he wasn't shivering when I opened up this morning, so it actually works.'

The rabbit hopped over to Anna, who immediately bent down and gave him a carrot that she'd brought in specially. 'You know, we really need to name him before we put him up for adoption.'

'I know. You think of something, Anna. I always go blank.' I still didn't like naming animals.

'I think the girls should name him. After all, he likes to sit with them when they're out here, and he hops around behind them all the time, doesn't he?'

'Okay, that's a good idea. They're away for the weekend but I'll ask them when they get home.'

'FLUFFY!' I looked at the bald rabbit, who was wearing a new, green woollen coat today, then at my four young daughters. 'You think we should call him Fluffy?'

I could see Anna was quietly choking with laughter behind her mug.

'Okay. Why Fluffy?' I asked all of them.

Lisa answered, 'Because he should be.'

There was logic after all. 'Right then – Fluffy it is. That's a nice name, thank you.'

Anna waited till they'd gone outside to play. 'Sorry, I had to laugh at first, but actually, that is quite a good name for a bald rabbit.'

Fluffy continued to live in the office, partly because he loved human company and was totally at home in there, and partly because there was no room for any more rabbits in the summer house at that time.

His next coat was in red and green stripes, with a small white bobble sewn onto the back of the neck, as it was Christmas. It was obvious that he'd been well loved by his owner at some point, because he was extremely friendly, and wasn't at all frightened when strangers went to stroke him. Edwina loved him, and spent as much time as I allowed her to, sitting in the office with him on her lap, or if it was dry outside, running around on the grass with Fluffy hopping along, kicking his back legs in the air every now and again as he followed her.

'All right, love?' I'd heard the office door open a bit, and looked up from my paperwork to see Lisa peeping through the gap.

'Edwina has asked me to write out a new Christmas list for her,' she said.

'Oh right. Have you done it?'

'Yes, it's here.' She came in and closed the door.

I looked at the new list and smiled. The first thing written on it was – FLUFFY. 'She wants Fluffy for Christmas?' I looked at my eldest daughter.

'She wants Fluffy, and a new yellow coat for him. I've told Grandma that she wants the coat and Grandma said she could knit one when she's at her own house so that Edwina doesn't see it.'

'What about the bicycle she asked for? Does she still want that?' I thought of the yellow bike that Tony had already hidden away in the back of the jumble shed.

'She would still like one, but she'd like Fluffy more. Can we go to the post box and post her letter to Father Christmas? She's waiting for me now.'

We were in the middle of nowhere, but there was a small post box just a few yards along the road. 'Hmm, okay, but be careful. I'll have a think about Fluffy. Thanks for telling me, love.'

I watched as Lisa took Edwina to post her letter.

By Christmas, Fluffy had grown a thin layer of new chocolate and cream fur, but a coat was still very necessary. He had several now, all in seasonal colours, and all with a little white bobble. I'd spoken to Tony and we'd agreed to let Edwina have him, as the two of them quite clearly loved being together. My mother had secretly knitted him a yellow coat, and embroidered his name in gold-coloured silk on the back of it.

On Christmas Eve, once the girls were asleep and we'd put the presents under the tree, we brought the four bikes out of their hiding places and leaned them against the sofa and chairs.

When everything was done, we stood in the doorway and I leaned against Tony as we looked at the array of presents. 'Merry Christmas, darling.'

He bent down and kissed the top of my head. 'Merry Christmas; I love you. Do you realise it's nearly one o'clock? The girls will probably be waking up soon.'

'Is it really? Come on – bed. You're right, they will be up at the crack of dawn.' We crept up the stairs.

'Open your eyes!' I pressed the button on the new video camera as the girls walked into the living room.

'Oh wow!' said Kelley, going straight to the green bike.

'Is that one mine, Mummy?' asked Shanie, pointing to the blue bike. The video camera nodded.

With a big smile on her face, Lisa went automatically to the red bike, which was much bigger than the other three.

Edwina stood in the doorway.

'What's the matter?' I asked her. 'Don't you like your bike?' I winked at Lisa, and handed her the camera.

Edwina walked towards her bike, and touched the handlebar. 'I do like my bike, Mummy.'

'But?' I prompted her.

'I asked Father Christmas for something else.' She looked at me solemnly.

Tony nudged my arm.

'Oh, did you? What was that then, love?'

Tony released Fluffy onto the floor, and he hopped straight into the living room towards Edwina. He looked resplendent in his yellow and gold coat.

Edwina squealed, and knelt down. 'Fluffy!' As he hopped up onto her lap, she looked at me, her eyes sparkling. 'He's what I asked for … Fluffy's what I asked Father Christmas for, Mummy.'

She put her arms around him and hugged him to her. 'I love you, Fluffy.'

The expensive yellow bike stood leaning against the arm of the chair, forgotten.

CHAPTER 14

Left to Die

Whenever Tony pulled up right outside the kennels, it was for a reason, so as he reversed up the driveway, I made my way down towards his van.

'Hello.' I looked around to see if there were any members of the public about. There weren't, so I leaned down and kissed him through the van window.

'Hello. Nice welcome.' He smiled.

'Nice husband.' I smiled back. 'What have you got in the back then?'

'A dog with a gammy leg.' He got out and opened up the back of the van.

A cream-coloured Lurcher sat quivering in the corner. 'Come on, Tilly,' Tony called as he untied her lead, but she didn't move.

'Tilly – that's a nice name.' I put my hand in towards her and let her sniff it, before stroking her ear.

'Hmm, shame her owner isn't as nice as her name. I've just picked her up from the bedsit where he abandoned her four days ago. Took all his belongings, and left the dog tied to a radiator by the bed.'

My blood started to boil. 'What a bastard.' I gently stroked down the side of her body. 'How come she was left until today then – I mean, if someone knew he'd buggered off four days ago, how come she wasn't found till now?'

'He told the man in the bedsit opposite that he was off, but didn't tell him that he'd left a dog tied up inside. It wasn't until the man heard whining coming from the empty room that he called the landlord, and when they broke in, they found the dog.'

'Jesus – what are some people like?' Tilly sniffed my hand and obviously decided I wasn't that bad, as she stood up, and slowly crept towards me. 'She's very thin, isn't she? Do you think we should give her several small meals a day instead of one big meal?'

'Good idea. I expect the vet would advise that anyway. There's something wrong with her right foreleg but the vet was out on an emergency so I said I'd bring her straight here and book her in to see him tomorrow.'

I noticed her leg as she approached the edge of the van. 'Oh God – it's bent. Oh – it looks awful, Tony, like it's broken or something.' The leg looked like the bow part of a bow and arrow, and made me feel physically sick.

'I thought that too. Like I said, I'll get her down to the surgery first thing in the morning. If it is a break, it's an old one, and by the look of it, it's never been properly set.'

'Bloody people … they make me sick. I suppose he's disappeared off the face of the earth, and will never have to pay for what he's done to her.' The lump in my throat grew bigger and more painful as she pushed her nose into my hand, and I looked into her brown eyes, wondering what sort of a life she'd had up until then.

'Unfortunately yes – he's disappeared. He'd only been in the bedsit for a few weeks, but the landlord had already started eviction proceedings because the man didn't come up with the rent money. When he checked with a previous address he found out the man had given him a false name, but someone fitting his exact description had left there a few weeks before, owing a lot of rent.'

'You know what? Working for the RSPCA is a real eye opener. I never dreamed there were so many arseholes living here; just here, in our own little bit of the world.'

I put my arm around the dog's neck and cuddled her.

We lifted Tilly out of the van, and she immediately shook her entire body, ending with the very tip of her whiplash tail.

'Come on Tilly, let's go and sort you out.' She followed me obediently, walking with a real dip, because when her bad leg touched the ground, it bent like rubber. It was so revolting my stomach churned and I had to stop looking.

She went obediently into the kennel. I wanted her to sit down, take the weight off that leg, but she stood at the door and watched me get her a bowl of water. I'd noticed some angry looking sore patches on her elbows and hocks, so got her a big thick blanket to lie on.

I expected her to wolf her food down, but she didn't; she ate in a very dainty manner, licking the bowl thoroughly when she'd finished. As I watched her, I saw a quiet, placid sort of dog, which just accepted everything that happened to it.

Next day, we found out a bit more. 'We were right. Her leg was broken, and never set properly, in fact, the bone was never set at all, according to the vet. He was surprised to see that she actually uses it. The bone has set itself, but very badly, and there are loose shards of bone around the injury too.' Tony shook his head.

'Oh God, how awful.' I imagined the pain that Tilly must have suffered. 'What does he think should be done? It can't stay like that – can it?'

'No. I have to take her back at eight-thirty in the morning. He says there are two options; one is to break the bone, tidy it up and re-set it – two, is to amputate the leg.'

'Amputate? That's a bit drastic, isn't it?' I raised my eyebrows.

'It is drastic, yes, and I've said I'd rather he tried to re-set the leg. He pointed out that it's not going to be cheap, but he agreed she should be given the opportunity of having full and proper use of it again if possible. Of course there are no guarantees, but at least he's prepared to try.'

'So – tomorrow is going to be a big day for her then.'

The next morning I waved to Tony as he drove off down the lane, and smiled at Tilly, who was sitting on the front passenger seat this time, with her head stuck out of the open window. I watched as her ears flapped about in the wind, and prayed that she would make it successfully through her big day.

It was a long day, despite all there was to do at the centre. At last, in one piece but a bit groggy, Tilly returned in the back of the van – and wagged her tail as I peered in at her! 'Hello, Tilly.' My voice squeaked as I subdued the familiar lump. 'My God – what the hell is that?' I pointed to the metal apparatus surrounding her leg.

'It's an external fixator, apparently. Or something like that.' Tony leaned in and picked up Tilly, complete with the blanket she was lying on. The broken leg, with all its paraphernalia, stuck out straight in front of him.

I went ahead and opened her kennel door. 'That's some contraption,' I said, as we manouvered Tilly and her leg through the kennel door. 'It must weigh loads. What's it all doing? Oh, daft question – I know what it's doing. I mean … why? Why has she got to have all that on her leg? I thought she'd come back with a plaster cast on it.'

'So did I, but the operation was complicated. I can't tell you exactly what the vet said because it was very technical. The gist of it though, was that the shards of bone were a problem, re-breaking the bone was a problem, and re-setting the bone was a problem. Is that good enough?' He looked at me.

I laughed at his description of what had happened. 'Okay. So – what do we have to do now?'

'Keep her as quiet as possible for the next couple of days. She's going to find it very hard to walk with it on her, and we may need to help her at first, but he says it's surprising how quickly animals get used to them.' He pointed to the framework of metal. 'This frame is holding pins in place, which have been inserted into the bone.' He touched one of the pins that disappeared into her skin. 'It was the only way that he could keep the bone together.'

'Oh Tilly.' I ran my hand along her rib cage. 'What have we done to you …?'

'Don't worry.' Tony put his hand on my back. 'She's going to be so much better off. Just think – she'll be able to run again.'

A mental picture of Tilly running across the field next door came into my head. 'You're right; she'll be so much happier – eventually.' I sighed as I closed the kennel door.

The next morning, as I opened up the block, Tilly was standing at the door of the kennel, wagging her tail.

'Wow! Hello you! Who needs our help then, eh!' I opened her kennel door and she limped out, dragging the metal-encased leg along as she went. Out on the grass, she didn't just wag her tail at me, she wagged her whole back end, and was so pleased to see me that I stayed and stroked her for a while. As she wasn't going anywhere fast I left her to it, and got the morning feeds ready.

The vet was impressed with her when he visited that afternoon. He hadn't expected her to move for at least a couple of days, and was surprised when I opened the kennel door and she walked out without any help.

'I've found out a bit more about Tilly's past,' Tony said, a couple of days later, as we watched her attempt to get hold of a ball that the girls were playing with.

'Tilly!' I scolded, and she obediently came towards me. 'How did you manage that?' I asked Tony. The dog crept off towards the girls again.

'I don't know if you've noticed the tattoo in her left ear? I wrote down the number, and checked it out. She was born in Ireland, and she's six years old. Unfortunately, that's all I've been able to find out, but at least we know her age now.'

'Well, well. Yes, I did notice it in her ear, but never thought anything about it. So – she's six. I thought she was older than that, so did the vet; he said about nine years. I wonder if she was brought over here by the same man who tied her up and left her.'

'I think she might have been,' Tony continued. 'I checked with the landlord again: the man had an Irish accent.'

A shiver went down my spine as I thought about him. 'The best thing he ever did for Tilly was tie her up to that radiator and sod off.'

Tony creased his brow as he looked at me. 'How on earth do you work that one out?'

'Because she's here now, with a leg well on the way to being normal again. If he hadn't abandoned her, where would she be? Tied up to some other radiator in some other bedsit, being starved, mistreated and left alone.' I took a deep breath.

'I see your point.'

The ball rolled towards us, and we both laughed as Tilly managed to run after it, on three legs, with the fixator being held out at an angle, and grab it.

'Oh stop it; it's not funny really. She's supposed to be taking it easy.' I called her over and took her back to her kennel. We ended up hiding all the balls, as every day when she was let out for a while, if she found one, she tossed it into the air and did her best to run after it.

Three weeks passed, and the day came when the external fixator was to be removed. I was excited, but also apprehensive. In all the time she'd had the contraption on her leg, she'd never put that foot down onto the ground.

I gave her a hug, and as I helped her onto the passenger seat in the van, looked across at Tony. 'Let me know as soon as you can? Love you.' I closed the gate behind them.

It was a horrible day. There was no phone call from Tony. A thunderstorm raged for ages and the rain was so heavy that even the covered dog runs were flooded. All the animals stayed huddled inside, except the geese and ducks which roamed the centre freely, and were busy dabbling in the waterlogged grass.

'Is she okay?' I called out as Tony reversed up the driveway, late that afternoon.

'She's fine.' Together we laid Tilly onto her bed.

As I fussed around, getting a bowl of tasty food, tucking the blanket in down the sides of the bed so there were was plenty of padding against the hard edges, I kept looking at her leg. It still stuck out straight, and was peppered with holes where the pins had been removed, but it looked normal.

She seemed more groggy than the last time, but still managed to wag half of her tail. She wasn't interested in the roast chicken that I'd cooked specially for her, so I put the bowl right next to her head. At least it was there if she wanted it. Her eyes closed, so I stroked her and left her to sleep.

'How did it go?' I asked Tony, who was sitting at the desk in the office, writing up his notes.

'Good. The vet's very pleased with everything. The X-ray shows that the bones have knitted together, so there's no reason why she shouldn't be able to do all the things a normal dog does – in time of course.'

'You have no idea what a relief it is to hear that.' I sat down opposite him. 'So, hopefully, within a few weeks she'll be ready for a new home? I can't let her go anywhere until she's completely fit.'

'It depends on how much she uses the leg. He doesn't want her doing too much at first, but realises it's going to be difficult to keep her quiet in a kennel environment. Perhaps you could put her up in the isolation unit for a while?'

'Okay; I suppose it would be better for the first few days. I'll sort out a kennel in there tomorrow. Anything we shouldn't do? Or shouldn't let her do?'

Tony thought for a moment. 'No. Just make sure she has as much peace and quiet as possible, and make her take it easy for a while – he's coming up tomorrow anyway, so if you've got any more questions, you can ask him then.'

'Oh well, it's just a matter of time then. I can't wait to see her running full pelt around the field.' I smiled to myself at the thought.

Tilly did her own thing with her leg; not using it at all for the first couple of days, then letting it just touch the ground. She didn't jump up in the kennel, and she only pottered about for a few minutes at a time. After a week, she was still putting most of her weight on the other foreleg, so she was following the vet's advice all by herself.

Another two weeks and things had moved on. She was much more confident, and put a good amount of weight on the leg as she walked. She was still on lead exercise only but her leg seemed to be getting stronger every day. I decided to put her up for re-homing.

All the animals available for homing were given a kennel card on which was written a brief personal history. Sometimes it was hard to know what to write, especially for a dog who'd been treated so badly, like Tilly.

Name: Tilly *Age*: 6 years *Sex*: Female

Reason for being here: Some bastard tied her up to a radiator and left her to die …

That's what I wanted to write, but obviously couldn't; it wasn't the 'done' thing.

So I'd end up writing something much more appropriate.

Reason for being here: Abandoned.

That was about as much as I could get away with, and at least I'd be able to tell people what had happened to her when they asked.

Tilly was a pretty dog, and bitches seemed to be easier to home than dogs. With the lovely temperament she had, and the fact that she was brilliant with children and cats, I knew it wouldn't be long before someone showed interest in her.

Mr and Mrs Baker turned up one Tuesday morning. They'd just lost their old dog, and were looking for another one. They didn't want anything young, they said, as they were no spring chickens themselves. Other than that, they didn't mind.

I showed them to the re-homing kennel block, and as we walked through the door, the first dog they saw was Tilly.

'That's the one,' said Mrs Baker, taking a hanky out of her handbag as she pointed to Tilly.

'Don't you want to look at any of the others?' I asked, somewhat surprised.

'No thank you.' She wiped the hanky across her eyes and blew her nose. 'That's the one.' She went to Tilly's kennel and put her hand through the bars.

Mr Baker beckoned me outside. 'Look,' he said, and showed me a photo of the dog they had just lost.

'Ah.' I smiled at him. 'Would you like me to get her out for you to see? It'll be less noisy outside.'

Mr Baker nodded and thanked me.

Tilly behaved perfectly, as I knew she would. She sat patiently next to Mrs Baker while I heard all about their previous dog; a cream-coloured Lurcher bitch, just like Tilly. After about ten minutes of listening to them both, it was obvious that they had adored their old dog, and they knew how to make a dog happy. The couple both stroked Tilly in between talking, and she licked each of their hands in return.

They are definitely the ones! I thought gleefully, and just knew that Tilly's luck was about to change. I wrote down all their details and arranged for a home-check to be carried out the following afternoon.

Just as I'd expected, the home-check was fine, and Mr Baker phoned to say they would be along first thing the next morning to collect her, as they needed to go out and buy some things for her first. I smiled at the sound of his excited voice. As I put the receiver down, I saw Tilly going off for a walk with one of the volunteers, and my smile grew bigger as I imagined how happy she was going to be in her new home.

'COME O-ON.' I called the goats for their afternoon feed, and waited, with their bowls in my hands, as the three of them trotted down.

'HELP. SOMEBODY … HELP!' a hysterical voice shrieked from the direction of the office.

I dropped the bowls of food and ran. The dog walker who'd gone out with Tilly a while before was outside, running around frantically; without Tilly. She stopped when she saw me.

'Where's Tilly?' I asked.

The girl sobbed. 'I had to leave her. I couldn't carry her. I tried …'

'WHERE'S TILLY?'

'Down the road, not far. I tried to carry …'

'WHICH WAY?' I screamed at her.

She pointed to the left. I got in my van and shot out of the driveway.

Tilly lay on her side, on the verge, but held her head up and watched as I approached. *Oh thank God, thank God, thank God … she's alive.* I screeched to a halt next to her, heart racing, stomach lurching.

Oh NO. Oh Tilly … I knelt down beside her and sobbed as I stroked her head.

Her leg. Oh God – she was holding her fixed leg up. Her fixed leg which was now broken. But not just broken; it was twisted sideways, with the end of the bone sticking out through the skin, dripping bright red blood down onto her rib cage. I sat up, put my hands to my cheeks and looked at the blood. Dripping … There was barely a second between each drip. At that rate, she could bleed to death.

For Christ' sake – pull yourself together. Get back to the centre. Call the vet. Close the centre. GO.

I carefully picked Tilly up and put her in my van.

My hand trembled as I picked up the phone. 'Hello, it's Jane from the RSPCA …'

The vet said he would be ready for her.

I noticed the dog walker, sitting on a chair in the corner of the office, quietly crying. She was only young, and I suddenly realised what a shock she'd just had too. I wanted to give her a hug, but couldn't; I was covered in Tilly's blood, so I called my Mum out to take care of her. Before leaving, I put the closed sign on the gate.

'Hello.'

I lifted my head off my arms and looked up to see Tony. 'Hello.' I'd cried so much I could hardly speak.

He sat down next to me and touched my cheek. 'You okay?'

'No.'

'Do you know how she is?'

'No.'

'Okay. I'll sit and wait with you.' He pulled one of the uncomfortable, waiting room chairs closer to mine, and sat down.

I turned to him and sobbed. 'Oh Tony … WHY? Hasn't she been through enough …'

'Hey.' He pulled my face up to look at him. 'I'm sure she'll be fine.'

'There was blood everywhere.'

He didn't seem to know what to say to that, so we just sat and waited.

It felt like hours before the door opened. My stomach lurched as we both looked up. The veterinary nurse stood there, with a smile on her face.

'The vet's just coming. I'm making tea – I need one after that. Would you like a cup?'

My face screwed up and my voice caught in my throat as I went to answer, but Tony said 'Yes, please.'

Over tea, the vet told us he'd had to amputate. Seeing her leg as I had, I didn't believe for a second that there was any other choice.

It had apparently been touch and go for a moment, but she was strong, and he believed she would pull through. She would be kept at the surgery for some time though.

We made our way back to our vans.

'Do you want to come in mine?' Tony asked. 'You can leave yours here until tomorrow, I'm sure they won't mind.'

I nodded. I didn't want to have to concentrate; I just wanted to go home.

It wasn't until Tony lit up two cigarettes that I realised it must have been hours since I'd had one, and I hadn't even wanted one. I decided to pack up smoking – later.

At eleven o'clock the next morning, I went to unlock the gate and hang the 'open' sign on it. With little sleep during the night, I was on automatic pilot.

'Good morning! We've come to adopt Tilly!' said Mr Baker.

I groaned. *How the hell could I have forgotten to ring them?*

'Good morning Mr Baker.' I managed a weak smile.

As I opened the gate, the couple followed me inside. They both talked to me at the same time, about what balls they'd bought for her, the colour of her new blanket … but all I could think about was what I now had to tell them.

'Would you like to sit down for a moment?' I offered them two chairs, then took a deep breath. 'There's been … a bit of an accident. Don't worry, Tilly's fine, but she's at the vet's.'

'Oh dear,' said Mr Baker. 'Could you tell us what happened?'

Phew … at least the worst bit's over.

'Yes of course. But first I'd like to apologise for not ringing you to save you the journey here today. Things have been a bit fraught. I'm just making tea, would you like a cup?' It'd been much easier to hear all the vet had to say, over a cup of tea.

They both wanted milk and two sugars.

Mrs Baker cried when I told her that Tilly's leg had been removed, and when I said I'd understand if they wanted to change their minds, as a dog with three legs wasn't necessarily going to be as easy to own as one with four legs, she assured me that she didn't care how many legs Tilly had – they were still going to adopt her.

We all laughed, and drank our tea.

'Can we still do the forms today, and adopt her officially?' asked Mrs Baker, as they stood up to leave.

I couldn't have said no, so the forms were completed. They also wanted to visit Tilly at the vet's, so that she got to know them, ready for when they took her home. The vet could be quite abrupt at times, but he understood how they felt, and was more than happy for them to visit.

Tilly never did come back to stay at the animal centre. Her new owners thought that she'd be better off straight to her new home from the vet's, and I totally agreed. A weekly call kept us in touch, and I looked forward to the day that they came to pay us a visit.

'They're bringing Tilly over today!' I told Tony. I'd visited her twice in her new home, when she'd still been recovering, but this was the first time I'd see her completely fit again. I'd asked them to come at lunch time, so that I could close the centre and walk in the field next door with them for a while.

Tony arrived home just before one o'clock. He was quietly excited; this was to be the first time he'd seen her since she'd left the vets.

'Hello!' Mr Baker stood by the office. 'We have a very excited dog here to see you!'

I grabbed a ball and Tony's hand, and put the closed sign on the gate. Mrs Baker opened the car door and Tilly leapt out, all wagging bum and whiplashing tail. She alternated between me and Tony, leaping up on her back legs, resting her one front leg on our stomachs. The lump arrived as I stroked her face, and I swallowed a few times to try and get rid of it.

'Can we take her into the field?' I asked the couple.

'Of course,' they both replied. Mrs Baker let Tilly off the lead, and the dog looked straight at me.

'She's seen the ball!' I laughed, and threw it for her.

As she loped across the grass, I couldn't believe how grace-ful she looked, or how quickly she ran. Within seconds, she was back again, and dropped the ball at my feet.

'You throw it.' I passed it to Tony, who could throw it much further than me, and off she went again.

She grabbed the ball and stopped. Her tongue was hang-ing out of the side of her mouth, her ears were pricked up, and she looked as if she had a smile on her face. My face crumpled as she trotted towards us.

'Are you all right?' Mr Baker touched my arm, concern written in his face.

'It's okay. Happy tears; they're just happy tears,' I said.

I took Tony's hand, and smiled up at him, and noticed that he had some happy tears too.

CHAPTER 15

It's Hard to Say Goodbye

'Why have you got your hand up the front of your jumper?'
I asked Tony.

'Hello to you too,' he responded, as he tried to squeeze
onto the armchair with Anna's dogs.

'You didn't actually answer my question.' I put my pen
down and waited.

He tried to push his bottom further back, but apart from
a grunt from one of the dogs, achieved nothing. With a sigh,
he gave up, and sat on one of the wooden chairs instead.

'You still haven't answered me.' I went and sat on the chair
next to him.

'I was trying to sit down.' He was a bit indignant.

'Well, at least it doesn't smell awful, whatever it is.' I
watched as he carefully brought his hand out into the open.

Curled up in his palm was a tiny, dark-coloured – thing. It
had no ears to speak of, just triangle-shaped flaps of skin that
were folded flat, closed eyes, and a rather large mouth. Its tail
was short, and it had four stumpy legs.

Fascinated, I took it from Tony and held it up. It squeaked
a bit and turned its head towards my hand. 'Well, I know it's

not a kitten, and I'm pretty sure it's not a puppy. I can see that it's a boy, but … okay, I haven't a clue, what is it?'

'A fox cub,' Tony replied. 'About three or four days old. There were two, but one of them died before I got there. There was a den in the back of a garden, and the people put a bit of fence around it to stop their Jack Russell from getting into it. They've been feeding the foxes for ages and were really pleased when they moved into the garden. They've got some amazing photos of the parents digging out their new home and playing together, as well as eating the food that had been put out for them.

'Unfortunately, little Jack dug under the fence this morning and got into the den. He came out with the two youngsters. The owners are devastated.'

'Oh God, I bet they are.' The cub twisted and turned in my hand, and pushed its nose into my skin. 'Bless it, it's hungry.'

'Ah. I've got all the stuff to feed him in the van.' He returned with a carrier bag full of bottles, teats and milk.

The bottles were the same shape as the one I'd used for the squirrels, but much bigger, and I found it difficult to cover the hole at the end with my thumb. As I tipped the bottle up to feed the cub, milk flowed everywhere except into his mouth, which I'd had to pry open – although he was hungry, he wasn't having any of it. After a lot of hassle and swear words, I gave up trying, and handed the fox cub back to Tony while I went in search of something else to use.

'Ah!' I pulled a 20ml syringe out of the medical box in the kitchen. 'Perfect!' I hurried back to the office.

The teat fit snug on the end of the syringe, but just to make sure it didn't accidentally come off and get swallowed by the cub, Tony bound it to the syringe with some strong cotton thread.

Finally, the cub lay, stretched out on my lap, with a belly full of milk. 'Tina is going to love you,' I whispered to him, as I stroked his side with one finger.

But Tina wasn't the only dog that was interested in the cub. Zara, my two-year-old German Shepherd, who had never shown the slightest interest in the baby squirrels, was transfixed.

'Look at her, Tony,' I laughed, that evening, as Zara stood, watching the cub being fed, with her head cocked to one side, her ears pricked forward and a sort of frown on her face.

He stroked Zara. 'Do you want to play mum this time?' Zara didn't take her eyes off the cub, but wagged the tip of her tail in response. Tina pushed forwards, and tried for about the fourth time to get a sniff of the cub. Each time she'd tried before, Zara had moved her body to block Tina, but not this time. Without a sound, Zara pulled her top lip back to expose a lovely set of teeth. Tina respectfully retreated.

'You know, she's never done that before.' I was a bit shocked that Zara had bared her teeth at the older dog. 'She's always been such a placid, laid back sort of dog. I'll have to sneak him to Tina when she's not looking.'

But there never was a time when Zara wasn't looking. I kept the fox cub in a cardboard box, next to the radiator in the living room, and it was as if she was glued to it. When I called the dogs to go out for a walk, when I fed them, even when we'd gone to bed the previous night, Zara wouldn't leave the cardboard box.

'I had to literally drag her out for a walk today,' I said to Tony, as I fed the cub the next evening. 'And half way round the field she disappeared. When I got back, there she was – in the living room, next to the box.'

'Strange, isn't it? She was never bothered about the squirrels, yet she won't even leave the cub to go for a walk,' Tony replied.

'Very strange.' I nodded as I put the cub on the floor for Zara to inspect. She pushed him around with her nose and sniffed, but didn't lick him once.

'You're no good, are you?' Tony told her, as she accidentally turned him upside down.

'Come on Tina, you're an old hand at this now, come and show Zara how it's done.' I picked up the cub and helped my overweight dog up onto the chair. There, much to Zara's annoyance, she spent several minutes giving the cub a thorough clean.

Two weeks later, the cub had grown well, and was even beginning to look like a fox. The girls loved watching Basil Brush on the TV, and were desperate to call the cub after the puppet, but I was adamant; it was a wild animal, going back into the wild when it was old enough, and it was not going to have a name.

'Hello Basil. I've heard a lot about you.' My dad poked the cub with his finger. He'd come over with Mum for Sunday dinner, and this was the first time he'd seen it.

The girls looked at me expectantly, waiting for me to start. I didn't disappoint them. 'It's not called Basil. It's a wild fox and it's going back into the wild so it …'

'Want a bit of ham, Basil?' Completely ignoring me, Dad got a sandwich bag out of his pocket, pulled a slice of ham out and pushed it in the cub's face.

I rushed towards the cub. 'It can't eat stuff like ...' I stopped, astonished, as the cub grabbed the ham, growled, and went under the front of the sofa with it. 'Oh.'

The girls all stood, silent, looking at the bottom of the sofa. My dad nudged Lisa and winked. 'Basil likes ham then.'

'Ted, you are awful.' My mother smiled at him, affectionately.

With my mother smiling, and my dad and the girls now in fits of giggles, I knew I'd lost the battle of the name and shrugged. 'Okay – I give in. Basil it is.'

The girls threw themselves on my dad as I went to make a cup of tea.

I'd had to move Basil out of his cardboard box after I'd found Zara in it with him. She had split the box all down one side, and wrapped herself round in a tight ball in what was left of it. Basil had been fast asleep on top of her.

A member of the public had donated an old wicker dog bed, and it fit nicely between the armchair and the fire, so I laid a thick blanket in it and called Zara. She wagged her tail but stayed where she was, with her nose under the edge of one of the armchairs, waiting for Basil to come out.

He spent most of his time play-fighting, usually with Zara's tail, and we marvelled at her patience with him. When he wasn't attacking her tail, he was leaping onto her head and biting her ears. She gave him the odd nip every so often, but most of the time she just put a paw on top of him, which flattened him successfully, until she was ready to let him go again.

Over time, I stopped all unnecessary human contact with Basil, as I was determined that he would be released back into his natural environment, and to help him learn about hunting, the wildlife rescue centre that we had come to rely on for advice suggested we start giving Basil day-old chicks to eat. Tony went to the local pet shop and came home with a frozen packet of twenty. I was mortified as I opened up the pack and took one out to defrost. I hadn't eaten meat for years, and although all of my family did, it was already disguised; already prepared, in cellophane wrapping, from a supermarket shelf.

I looked at the frozen, dead chick and felt the most awful guilt, but had to console myself with the fact that if Basil was to survive in the wild, then like other carnivores he would have to kill; anything he could. I put the chick in a cat bowl on top of the cupboard, behind some tins of food, so it was out of sight.

'Will you give Basil this chick?' I asked Tony, when he got home.

He took the chick and went into the living room. Basil was trying to shred one of Zara's ears, so Tony picked him up by the scruff of his neck and carried him out into the garden. 'Come on, you little tyke.' He put the wriggling cub on the ground and held the chick in front of his nose.

'Bloody hell.' I was really shocked. Basil leapt at the chick and growled ferociously in his high-pitched, puppy type way as he tugged it.

'Look at him – that's his real fox instinct kicking in,' said Tony.

Tony played tug for several seconds, then let Basil have the chick. The cub ran off through the front door, back into the living room.

'No! I don't want him eating defrosted chicks in the house – there'll be bits!' I ran off after him, while Tony stood and laughed.

Some minutes later, after moving all the heavy furniture around to find him, he appeared from the little gap behind the wicker dog bed, sat on Zara, and cleaned his paws.

Tina stopped cleaning his bits the day he playfully bit her on the nose. She nipped him back hard for doing it and made him yelp, and that was the end of their relationship.

Zara, on the other hand, followed him everywhere, and if he strayed too far for her liking, she picked him up by the scruff and carried him back into the living room. As soon as she let him go, he'd shoot off again, and she'd trot patiently after him and repeat the process. I was reminded of Tina with the squirrels, and knew that the time was approaching when the cub would have to leave.

'We need to find somewhere for Basil to be rehabilitated soon,' I said to Tony, after he'd run amok in one of the girls' bedrooms. 'Somehow, he managed to get up onto the windowsill and knock all the dolls down. Then he chewed the heads on two of them, and the legs on another one. He's pulled the arm off one of the teddy bears, and the stuffing is all over the floor, and he's poo'd on one of the beds.'

'Oh dear. I'll ring the wildlife centre tomorrow, and see what I can arrange. They did say that they were inundated with cubs when I rang them, so I don't know if they've got any room there, but I'm sure they will be able to give us the phone number of someone who can take him.' He stopped and smiled as Basil rushed into the kitchen and started attacking the mop.

'I hope so,' I said, as I pulled him off the mop. I held him up in front of me and watched him as he wriggled and tried to get down. 'He's nearly seven weeks old now, and it's definitely time for him to learn to be a proper fox. I think between us and Zara, we've given him a good start, but now that he's older, he does need to be with other cubs.' I put him back on the floor and he promptly leapt up and grabbed the end of the oven gloves that were hanging down over the side of the cupboard.

'Oh Basil,' said Tony, laughing as the cub disappeared through the doorway, with my oven gloves trailing behind.

That year was apparently a bad one for fox cubs, and all of the wildlife rehabilitation centres were overflowing with orphans to the extent that they just couldn't take any more.

'What the hell are we going to do?' I asked Tony, after he'd been told there was no room at the fourth centre he'd phoned.

'I honestly don't know. They've just given me the number of a place in the Midlands, but they aren't sure what the situation is with foxes there at the moment, so it could be another no. At least I can phone them and find out.'

Two minutes later it was another no.

'This is ridiculous. What are we going to do with him if we don't find somewhere? I'm not keeping him, Tony, no matter what – I'm not keeping a wild fox in a cage. He disappeared for ages yesterday, and I finally found him down the lane, pouncing on a frog. He could easily have been run over, or got lost. The foxes around here would probably kill him if he was out in their territory at night; he's way too small to look after himself. He's a complete outsider, and wouldn't stand a chance.'

I was getting really worried about Basil's future now, which wasn't something I'd bargained on when we were still bottle-feeding him just a couple of weeks before.

Tony looked at me. 'There is one thing we can do, but it's not something I'd choose; take him to a sanctuary …'

I had a bit of an edge to my voice when I replied. 'WHAT! You must be bloody joking. There is no way on this earth that I'm putting a WILD, healthy, perfect, young fox cub into a bloody cage for the rest of its life.' I stormed outside.

A while later Tony appeared, and sat on the door step next to me. 'Are you okay?'

'Oh God – I'm so sorry.' I rested my head against his arm. 'Sanctuaries do have their place in the scheme of things; like I've said before, I'd love to run one myself, one day – but I don't want to put Basil into one. He's got his whole life ahead of him, and I want him to live it naturally. I just can't believe how difficult it is to find someone who has the room to rehabilitate him. Just one little fox cub …'

After another possibility at another centre was dashed, even Tony had begun to lose hope of finding somewhere for Basil, then, out of the blue, he was told about a woman in the New Forest who only took in and rehabilitated foxes. I sat, anxiously waiting, as he dialled her number.

'Hello there. My name's Tony. I'm an RSPCA Inspector, and I've been given your number by a bird rescue centre. We have a young fox cub, about eight weeks old now, and need to find somewhere for him. We've tried several centres but they're all overflowing with cubs and can't take ours. I wondered if you would be able to help?'

At least two minutes went by and Tony remained silent as the woman talked. My hopes were raised when he said, 'Yes, he eats day-old chicks, and we give him raw bones with meat on them, as well as tinned dog food,' but dashed within seconds when he said, 'Oh … I see.'

I got up and paced the office floor.

Another minute – another word from him, 'Okay.'

Oh for God's sake … come on, this is his last chance of going back into the wild …

I lit a cigarette, and carried on pacing.

'Yes, I understand. Thank you very much, goodbye.' He replaced the receiver.

'She can't take him, can she?' I stopped and looked at him.

'Ever the pessimist, you.' He shook his head at me as he reached for a cigarette.

'Well, can she then?'

He lit his cigarette.

'Oh for God's sake – why do you do this to me! Can she take him or not?'

'Yes.'

I flopped onto the chair, and heaved a massive sigh of relief. 'Well, that's all right then.'

Two days later, we set off for the New Forest with Basil.

'Stop it, you little fiend.' I leaned round the car seat and pushed Basil's nose back in through the wire of the cat basket. 'He's making his nose sore on the top where he keeps trying to chew his way out of the basket.'

Tony looked round at him briefly. 'Not much longer now, hopefully. We're in the New Forest, but the place we're going is apparently not the easiest of places to find. The woman has given me directions, but she was unsure about one of the roads herself, so we may have to stop and ask people as we go.'

'The sooner the better is all I can say.' I stopped Basil for the second time, but within minutes he was worrying the wire again, and making an agitated noise as he did.

After another hour of trying to prevent the cub from making his nose even worse, and with an ache in my back from spending so much time twisted sideways, we pulled up outside a forlorn-looking cottage. The name on the wall plaque had lost a nail, and hung lopsidedly, but it was still readable.

I looked at Tony. 'Welcome to Rose Cottage,' I whispered, as he knocked on the front door.

It was ages before the door opened, and the lady that greeted us wasn't at all what I was expecting. She must have been in her seventies, and her back was quite badly hunched over. I noticed her arthritic fingers as she pulled open the warped front door. She led us down a long, gloomy hallway, and I made an instant decision; Basil was not staying there.

'This way, my dears,' she said as we took a left turn into the kitchen. The sink was covered in thick cobwebs, from the once-gold taps to the plug hole, where a huge brown spider sat waiting.

I shivered involuntarily as we walked through. *What a complete waste of time. All this way for nothing. Oh Basil …*

'Did it take you long to find us?' the lady asked Tony.

We headed into the garden, which was surprisingly organised, with a neat little vegetable patch along the edge of the cut grass.

'About an hour, once we were in the Forest, but at least we did find you.' He smiled at her. 'How many cubs have you got at the moment?'

'Seven – and Basil will make eight,' she laughed.

Oh no he bloody won't. I bristled at the thought.

We walked for a couple of minutes before passing through a strong, wire gate which had chain-link fencing attached on either side. The fencing was virtually covered in undergrowth, and I noticed the surroundings becoming more wild – more overgrown, except for the well beaten path that we were following.

'Here we are then; this is where they will be released, but not until they're about five months old though. I've been poking around here every day for the last few weeks, just to see if there is any fox activity, and there hasn't been a single one around. Just the right spot for my youngsters.' She walked over to a pile of logs, stacked a good three feet tall, and went round behind it.

We followed.

She lifted a log, and took a torch from its hiding place underneath. 'Saves me keep bringing it with me. I have my hands full enough with all the food.'

Tony and I looked at each other, nonplussed.

She moved further round the pile and got to what looked like a door, on a sideways angle. It folded right back and revealed a small cavern-type space inside the log pile. 'Come in, come in, it's quite safe.' She beckoned us inside with the torch.

In wonder, I crouched down and walked under the logs.

'I'll stay out here,' said Tony. 'I don't think I'd fit.' He laughed.

'All right then.' The woman smiled at him. 'I can tell you about it while you're standing out there. I just like to show people what I do, and how I do it.'

She told us how she'd had it specially built, with the logs outside to make it look more natural. That way, the cubs she released had the most natural surroundings that they could, while still being contained until they were about five months old, behind the chain-link fencing that we had seen on the way.

That particular log pile was just one of four that she'd had built on her land, and each was quite a way from the next. There were still foxes that she'd released in previous years living in two of the other log piles, but badgers had taken over the third, so she wasn't able to use it at that moment.

I had to admit, I was beginning to warm to this woman. She certainly knew what she was talking about, and in my frequent daydreams about Basil's future, I'd always sent him to live somewhere – like this.

Then she ruined it.

'Would you like to see the other cubs? They're all in the play pen, at home.'

Straight away, I imagined Basil, sitting patiently in a play pen of the lobster variety, in a gloomy, cobwebby room. *Oh …*

We followed her back along the path, but way before we reached the cottage, turned off the main path and went towards a high, neatly cut privet hedge. It was like walking into the secret garden; beautiful flowers, vibrant colours, heavenly scents everywhere.

I couldn't help gasping loudly as I looked around me.

'Beautiful, isn't it?' She smiled at me. 'I have a very good gardener. He happens to be quite a good husband too.'

I laughed, and for the first time, relaxed, and made an instant decision; I was completely wrong about my first instant decision. This was where I wanted Basil to be; to have his chance – to live his life as he should – even if he had to spend a bit of time in a play pen first.

'The cottage has severe structural problems, and has to be pulled down,' she was telling Tony, as she gave him a mug of coffee. 'We knew when we bought it, oh, more than ten years ago now, and we put this mobile in – just until we had made up our minds what to do.' She flourished her hand at the air. 'And we've lived here very happily, ever since.'

I looked around the cosy little living room, and understood how she felt.

'Now, let me show you the other cubs.' She led the way to another gate.

Once through, we found ourselves inside a huge wire pen, with little log piles and tree stumps dotted all over the place. Patches of ivy grew up the wire, and rhododendron and hydrangea bushes hid a small shed. As we moved towards it, a cub ran across in front of us, and disappeared under one of the piles. Two more cubs tumbled out from behind one of the bushes, play fighting, then scrambled through a hole in the side of the shed.

The play pen!

The woman stopped when she got to the shed, and turned to us. 'Most of the youngsters haven't had any human contact for a while now, which is how it must be if they are to survive in the wild. One or two of them may approach you, but I'd appreciate it if you ignore them.' Tony and I nodded.

She slowly pulled open the shed door, and in the dimness, we could just make out four cubs, sitting scrunched up together against the back wall. 'They were all hand-reared, five of the seven, by me, but they are already learning to keep away from humans. They must learn this, because we are their only real, natural enemy. Not everyone wants foxes in their back gardens.' She shook her head as we left the play pen.

'Right.' Tony smiled at her. 'Thank you so much for showing us around, it's been very enlightening. And thank you for agreeing to take Basil. We could never have given him this kind of opportunity.' He looked at me. 'I think it's time to get Basil.'

My stomach lurched as I realised this was it. I was about to say goodbye to the little creature that had made such a huge impression on me, and my family – and it hit me properly that I was never going to see him again.

Tony opened up the back door of the van. Basil was still chewing on the meaty bone we'd given him, and he growled at Tony as he put his hand into the basket.

'Come on, Basil.' Tony picked him up, and pulled the bone off him, before following the woman back to the play pen. Basil struggled all the way, but Tony held firm, and didn't put him down until we were right inside the pen. I expected him to leap off and attack something, but he didn't; he stood next to us and trembled. I bent down and stroked him; I needed to hide the tears that were now flowing, and he jumped up onto my lap and hid his head under my arm.

Oh Basil … this isn't how it's supposed to be. I had to wipe my tears, not wanting anyone to see I was crying; not the woman anyway. *Goodbye, little one. Be brave.* I put Basil back on the ground. I sniffed.

'Time to go.' Tony took my hand. We walked away from Basil. The woman followed, but said nothing. Basil never moved. The pain I felt inside was like nothing I'd ever felt before. There'd be no visits. This was goodbye for ever.

At the gate, I turned, expecting him to be right behind me, but he'd been spotted by another cub, who'd gone up to him and was sniffing his nose. We watched from outside as the other cub put a paw on his face.

A second cub ventured out of the shed and walked slowly towards him, before suddenly grabbing his tail. Basil shrieked and turned on the cub, which leapt off after a leaf being blown along by the wind. I smiled through my tears; it was just the sort of thing Basil did all the time.

The first cub pawed at his face again, and licked his ear, and Basil copied, and licked that cub's ear. Tony passed me a hanky as my tears really began to flow.

'He doesn't need us any more; he needs them now.' Tony nodded his head towards the play pen.

'I know.' I broke down, and sobbed into his hanky. I didn't care what the woman thought any more. 'It's just so hard, saying goodbye.'

A yelp drew our attention back to the cubs, and I laughed, a bit hysterically, as I watched Basil leap on the back of a bigger cub and pretend to kill it.

The cub that had licked his face joined in, and a rough and tumble between the three of them ensued. After a minute or so, Basil stopped and looked around. He saw us on the other side of the wire, and bounced over to us. I put my fingers through a small gap, and stroked his nose. *Take care Basil, I love you.* He licked me, then ran off towards the two that were once again engaged in play fighting, and leapt in.

'Come on, let's go.' Tony held his hand out to me.

'Yes. It is time to go now.' I took his hand as we turned and walked away from Basil for the very last time.

CHAPTER 16

Let's Have a Jumble Sale!

I couldn't find Anna or Marie anywhere. 'ANNAA.'

'YO,' shouted Marie.

The shed; I hadn't even thought to look in the shed where we stored all the donated blankets, clothing, and other unwanted items that people thought might be useful to us.

'Here you are.' I peered into the gloom at the back of the twenty-foot-long shed, and saw them both almost at ceiling level, perched on top of piles of dustbin bags. I held up two mugs of tea.

'You – are a lady,' said Marie, as she slid and climbed over everything to get to me.

'Oo, thank you. Have you seen this lot?' said Anna. 'We had a big van turn up yesterday, full of clothes and stuff. He said they're emigrating and his wife is being brutal because of the cost of shipping it all over to Australia.'

'Yeah,' said Marie. 'It would have cost Loadsamoney!'

Anna and I groaned; it was Marie's favourite saying, thanks to a revolting TV character.

'No I hadn't. Blimey, there's a lot, isn't there?' I picked up a jumper that had fallen out of the top of one of the bags, and held it up against me. 'Hey, that's a really nice jumper. It seems such a shame to use it as bedding for the animals.'

'I know,' Anna replied. She pulled a child's dress out of another bag, and held it up. 'Look at this; it's brand new, and it's still got the price tag on it.'

'Ah, but look at this.' Marie knelt up on the bags, and tied the straps of an apron round her neck and waist. It was the body of a hunky man, and we burst out laughing as she lifted a flap of material where the underpants would have been, and revealed a little something.

After rummaging around for a few minutes, we'd found lots of items of clothing which had obviously never been worn. Marie had also found some cardboard boxes full of ornaments, perfumes, toys, and various items – all new, or in very good condition.

To get a better look at it all, I climbed over everything to where the window was supposed to be, and pulled some bags away from it to let in a bit of light.

'That's better,' said Anna, as she held up a carved elephant ornament.

That's beautiful,' I said. 'God – what are we going to do with it all?'

Anna smiled. 'I know … let's have a jumble sale!'

'Oh yeah – brilliant idea, Mater!' said Marie.

I looked at Anna. 'You are joking, aren't you?'

'Oh come on – think of all the money we could make; we need a new washing machine for a start,' she replied.

'Go on, woman. We could make Loadsamoney.' Marie grinned. 'It'd be great fun. Tony could do some sausages and burgers too. He's good at the old barbecue stuff, isn't he? Not too much gets burnt ...'

I threw a pillow case at her.

Anna continued, 'Seriously, we could make some money for the animal centre and it's not going to cost anything. And you're right, Marie – a barbecue at the same time would be fun, and another money spinner.'

Marie didn't hear; she was too busy holding a small glass pot and lid up to the light.

I was beginning to warm to the idea. 'We'd need tables to lay all the stuff out on, and people; we'd need people to help us get everything ready, and then to sell it, and we'd need to sort it into some kind of order, you know – kids' clothes on one table, women's clothes on another. Then there are all the ornaments and other things. It would take ages to put it out everywhere. We'd have to buy the burgers and buns, and sort out a barbecue ... Oh, I don't know.' I was talking myself out of the idea.

Anna didn't give up easily. 'I know someone who would be able to organise it all ...'

'But it would take them ages; would they want paying do you think?'

'Noo, she loves doing things for people. Tell you what – if you agree, I'll go and see her after work, and if she agrees, we'll do it.' She looked at me expectantly.

I hesitated. 'Oh ... I don't know, all right then.'

Marie shrieked. 'Yey! We're having a jumble sale!' Then more quietly, said, 'I have found a seriously nice writing set thingy. It should be worth Loadsamoney. Can I take it to the antique shop in town and see what they say?'

'Of course you can,' I replied, laughing at her. 'But don't be too disappointed if it isn't worth Loadsamoney.'

Anna pretended to scream. 'Bloody hell, don't you start!'

Marie winked at me.

The next morning Anna told me the woman would be delighted to organise everything, and had already spoken to some friends of hers about helping. She would need to know the date as soon as possible though.

'Hmm.' I thought for a moment. 'How about in a couple of months – say, August, just to make sure she has plenty of time.'

'A couple of months? How about in a couple of weeks? It isn't going to take much to arrange it all,' Anna replied.

'Oh, okay. A couple of weeks. Are you sure that's long enough? There's so much to do …'

Anna smiled at me. 'Don't worry, she knows what she's doing. Jane, are you sure you want to have a jumble sale? I feel like me and Marie have bulldozed you into this, and if you aren't happy about it – I can tell the woman we've changed our minds.'

'Oh, don't mind me, Anna – I'm just being cautious, but I am happy about it, and I do want us to do it. I just want it to be a success.'

Anna squeezed my arm. 'It will be a success; I promise you.'

Patty met Anna at the centre the following Monday morning to see what we had, and decide what needed to be done. She was surprised at how much stuff we had piled up in the shed, and at the quality of it, and said she knew we'd do well.

She came each day for the rest of that week, and brought friends with her, who brought tables with them. They spent hours sorting through everything, putting different piles on different tables, before bagging it up and labelling it.

Anna had already put an advert in the local paper, and we'd had call after call from people, wanting more information, or offering more goods to sell. I began to get excited.

'This is better than having an open day, isn't it?' I said to Anna, as we carried all the bags and boxes out onto the grass, ready for the women. 'Just think how good it'll be if we make enough money for a washing machine!'

'I think we will. And maybe a bit more, with the barbecue as well. Has Tony decided what he's cooking the food on?'

I giggled. 'Oh, you should see what he's done. He's got hold of an old oil drum and cut it in half. He's stacked up breeze blocks and made two cradles for the drum halves to sit on, and then got a big bit of that strong half-inch-square wire that we used for the chicken pen to cook the food on.'

'I knew he'd come up with something.' Anna laughed. 'Where's he going to put it?'

'We thought that it would be better to keep it away from all the tables because of the smoke, so he said about going up between the tree and the summer house. The grass will be clear of tables there, so people can sit down to eat if they want.'

'Good idea. And I'm going to be his first customer,' she said, rubbing her stomach.

People that I'd never seen before turned up and asked for Patty, as they'd come to help with the sale. By four o'clock that afternoon, the place was teeming with volunteers, and I could only watch as, under Patty's direction, the tables went up and the goods went onto them.

The clothes were at the end of the driveway nearest the gate; men's, then women's, then children's, covering six long tables. Kitchen and household items filled three tables on the way up into the centre. Around the grassed area, another eight tables were laid out. One had a mixture of perfumes, talcum powders and bath products, two were covered in children's toys, another had books stacked on top of each other, and the remaining four were full of ornaments. Very nice ornaments.

I walked slowly around the tables, and grinned to myself. I was going to enjoy this.

As with the open day, we didn't want to charge an entrance fee, and we decided that instead of shaking buckets at people on the way in, we'd leave buckets outside the office for people to throw money into on the way out – if they had any left of course.

At five minutes to six, Marie went down to the gate and started talking to the group of people gathered at the front of the queue. Nerves were getting the better of me, as I checked the tea, milk and sugar for the umpteenth time. I knew it was all there, but had to check just to make sure. I realised I'd probably overdone it with the orange squash: there were fifteen bottles stored under the table, just in case we got through the ten on the table. That was excluding the five bottles of lemon.

Tony was quite happy. He had loads of charcoal, burgers, sausages, rolls and ketchup, and he'd bought a new set of barbecue tongs.

A table behind him held all the rolls and serviettes, and as I went to see if he was okay, he was at the table, cutting rolls.

'Hello, you all set?' I asked him.

He turned – and I nearly died. He was wearing the hunky man apron.

'What *are* you wearing?' I hissed. 'Take it off!' My employers were mainly elderly ladies, who had been elected onto the committee that ran the animal centre. At least four of them were here, and I wasn't quite sure how they would take it.

'What's wrong?' Tony smiled. 'Don't you like my apron?'

'Take. It. Off. NOW.' I glared at him and made a mental note to kill Marie.

'Hello darlings!'

Hell …'Hello, Audrey.' I turned round to see one of my elderly employers, puffing a long, expensive cigarette through an even longer, solid gold cigarette holder. 'It's nice to see you.' I moved away from Tony, hoping she would follow me.

'Hawhaw! Divine, Tony – absolutely divine!' I looked round to see Audrey, holding up the flap on Tony's apron.

Well! Who'd have thought … I looked at Tony, cringed, and left them guffawing together.

Marie opened the gate, and there was an influx of people. An elderly couple made straight for my refreshment table, so I ran over to them. *Here we go then.*

'Good evening! What would you like?' From that moment, I didn't stop.

I saw Marie regularly throughout the next two and a half hours. Apart from running round with cups of tea I'd made for the stall holders, she helped the older people carry things back to their cars, took burgers and sausages to people who were already sitting on the grass, and talked to children of all ages about toys their parents had bought for them.

Now, at the end of the evening, she stood at the gate, doffing her hat at everyone, thanking them for coming, and saying she hoped they'd spent Loadsamoney while they were there. I decided I didn't want to kill her after all. In her check shirt and braces and Doc Marten boots, she looked 'well hard', as she used to say, but she had the softest heart, and as I watched her, I hoped that my girls would turn out as well as she had.

'Phew! What an evening!' said Anna, when all the people had finally gone home. The sun was just setting, and the clouds had a beautiful pink tint as we all gathered round one of the tables to watch Patty and some of her helpers count the money. I handed out tea as we waited.

Anna grabbed my arm. 'Look at it all, Jane! We've done really well, haven't we?'

I was definitely getting more emotional as I got older, as that old lump in my throat was there, again. I swallowed several times and coughed. 'We have done well, Anna; I'm so chuffed.' I looked around at all the people, and didn't know how I was going to thank them for all the effort they'd put in.

'Hey!' Marie held up a big wad of notes and shook it. 'We have made … LOADSAMONEY!'

A big cheer went up, and people that I'd never met before that day turned to me and shook my hand, as if I'd done it all myself.

'Marie! Everyone wants to know how much we've actually made!' said her mother.

Marie grinned. 'The actual amount that we have made is: Two … hundred … and forty five poundsandseventytwopence! Ta da!'

Another big cheer went up, and this time, everyone congratulated everyone. Anna and I thanked everyone for all their help, and presented Patty with a box of chocolates that we'd bought ourselves. Slowly, they all made their way back out to their cars.

Tony wandered around the centre with me and the girls the next morning, picking up the bits of litter that we'd missed in the dark the evening before. I was still on a high from the amount of money we'd made. A washing machine was definitely going to be bought with the proceeds, and there should still be some left over.

Marie opened the gate, and Anna drove in. Her dogs jumped out before her, and her greedy crossbreed, Brodie, straight away found half a sausage wrapped in a serviette. He didn't bother to unwrap it.

It was still early, so we sat with a cup of tea and talked about the success of the jumble sale.

'Actually – I've got some good news,' said Marie, as she stood up and took a money bag from her jeans pocket. 'I took that writing desk thingy to the antique shop in town. They told me it was from the seventeen hundreds. The little cut glass inkwells that sat in the little holes in the wood were the originals, and even the hinges on the lids were still in excellent condition.'

Anna grinned and nodded.

Something big was coming.

'So, I asked them how much it was worth,' said Marie.

We waited.

Anna nudged her. 'Go on; tell them.'

A huge grin spread over Marie's face. 'They said it was worth … LOADSAMONEY!'

I burst out laughing. 'Marie, I do love you!'

Anna shoved her. 'Bloody tell them!'

'Okay Mater. They gave me … two … hundred … and eighty quid!' she finished, and sat back down.

I was stunned. 'Really?'

Marie laughed. 'Yes, really.'

Tony looked at her and very seriously said, 'Marie, that is amazing. It's a good job you realised its potential value. Well done. You've made the animal centre Loadsamoney.'

Marie doffed her hat to him and winked.

'Christ,' I said, and hugged her.

Anna sat back on her chair, obviously pleased with what her daughter had done.

Tony took Marie into town, and they bought a good quality washing machine. They also bought a tumble dryer, and a new fridge freezer, as the freezer part on our old one hadn't worked properly for ages. Once they'd finished, they looked at the change they had, and bought bones for all the dogs, fresh chicken to cook for all the cats, carrots for the rabbits, and three loaves of brown bread for the goats, ducks and chickens.

When they showed us their shopping, we both laughed, and sighed with happiness.

It was lunch time, and I was looking for Anna. 'ANNAA.'

'YO,' called Marie.

I should have known; the shed.

As I looked inside at the pair of them, sitting on top of a pile of dustbin bags, I realised just how much stuff we still had left. I handed Marie their mugs of tea.

'Blimey, there's still loads in here, isn't there?' I said. 'What on earth are we going to do with it all?'

'I know,' said Anna, with a huge grin on her face. 'Let's have a jumble sale …'

CHAPTER 17

The Quiet Day Off

'Cock a doodle doo … Cock a doodle doo … Cock a dood …' I slammed my hand down on top of the annoying alarm clock that my father had bought me for Christmas.

'Ohh.' I really didn't want to get up. As I moved, Trix poked her head out from under the quilt, sniffed the chilly air, and went back under. She didn't seem to want to get up either.

'Come on,' I said to her, and pulled the quilt back. As I put my feet on the carpet, she stretched, and rolled over onto her back. 'Go on, get up.' I shoved her gently.

The dogs went in front of me down the stairs, wagging their tails. They knew the routine; out for a wee, and after that a bowl of tea.

I opened the door and put the kettle on.

'LISA, KELLEY, SHANIE, EDWINA … TIME TO GET UP,' I shouted up the stairs. Silence followed, as always.

The tea was brewing in the pot, the dog bowls were lined up on the floor, the mugs on the cupboard. I was just pouring the milk, when I heard an almighty ruckus outside. With nothing on my feet, and still in my pyjamas, I rushed out to see what was going on.

My heart missed a beat when I realised that a massive dog fight was in progress.

'TONY,' I screamed, as I ran towards the melee, but he'd already heard it and was right behind me.

He ploughed in and grabbed his German Shepherd, April, pulled her clear, and shoved her into the dog run next to the office. I grabbed Zara, and after a struggle, managed to get her into the run with April. Tony had already gone back in and was trying to get hold of Tina, but she was on her back being attacked by a St Bernard that we'd never seen before. Hands covered in slobber from the big dog, he tried to get it off Tina, but it was so huge and so preoccupied with killing Tina, it didn't even notice. A German Shepherd I'd never seen before was also going for Tina, so I grabbed its tail, screamed abuse at it, and pulled with all my might. As it let Tina go and turned, Tony grabbed its scruff and dragged it into the next run.

The St Bernard was shaking Tina by the chest as if she was a rag doll, and no matter what we did, she wouldn't let go. Tina was still trying to bite the dog, even though it had its teeth sunk into her rib cage.

Hose pipe – get the hose pipe. I ran up to the top of the kennel blocks and turned the tap on. As I ran back down, the hose pipe unwound. I twisted the nozzle, and pointed it at the St Bernard's face. It ignored the water for a few seconds, but I aimed the strong jet right into its mouth, and it choked, and let Tina go. Tony pounced on it immediately, yelled 'NO' and started dragging it along. It struggled, but he held firm and shoved it into the run with the German Shepherd.

I dropped the hose, which snaked around until it rested against the hedge. It continued to gush water right across the driveway. Tina was lying on the ground, yelping. 'It's okay, it's okay.' I cradled her head in my arms and tried to calm her down. I looked at Tony, who was bent over double trying to get his breath after dragging the St Bernard into the run.

'Have you seen Trix anywhere?' I asked him.

He stayed bent over, but shook his head.

Tina had stopped yelping but hadn't tried to move, so I carried on sitting with her, but I felt anxiety rise up in my stomach; I needed to find Trix.

She must have heard me say her name, because she crept out from under the privet hedge – in one piece, with her tail very much between her legs, and tried to climb onto my lap as I held Tina.

Oh thank Christ …

I lifted my arm and she settled with her head underneath it, and I carried on sitting there for a while, in a daze.

'Mummy – what's happened?' asked Lisa.

I had no idea how long she'd been standing there, in her nightie. 'It's all right, love, just a bit of a fight with two dogs that are in the run now. Tina's shocked I think, but she'll be fine.' Tina wasn't the only one who was shocked.

'Shall I make the tea then?'

'Oh, that would be lovely, thank you. Could you do me a big favour? Go and get the other three up? I don't want them to be late for school.'

'Okay. Do you want me to take Trix in and give her some tea?'

'Yes please. Can you manage her? I don't think she'll walk in.'

'I can carry her.' Lisa picked her up. 'Come on, Trix.'

'Let's get Tina indoors.' Tony had his breath back again.

I looked up at him and had to smile. He was wet through, and still had slobber on the back of one of his hands. I didn't look much better. 'Look at the state of us. Anyone would think we'd just sorted out a dog fight.'

He looked down at me. 'How can you be so jovial, after that?' He offered me his hand. 'Come on, I need a coffee before I can smile.' He pulled me up.

Tina hadn't moved, so Tony pushed her over and she sat up. He patted her on the head. 'Come on; let's see if you're okay.'

I looked around at the ground. 'There's no blood, surprisingly, but I suppose that doesn't mean anything, does it?'

'That's the trouble, she might have internal injuries. I think it would be best to get her checked over, just in case,' Tony replied.

'Okay. You're probably right.' I didn't really want to have to put Tina through a vet check as she was one of those dogs that had a real fear of going to the surgery.

As we stood, either side of her, deciding whether to put her straight into the back of Tony's van, she got up, shook herself, and waddled over onto the grass. After a quick sniff, she had a wee, then waddled back indoors.

We looked at each other, and Tony managed a smile.

'Ah! You don't need coffee before you smile, after all,' I teased him, and took his arm. He smiled more, and gave me a kiss.

We followed Tina in, and found her sitting in the kitchen, watching Lisa, who was dishing out tea to children and dogs. Lisa gave her a bowlful, and she guzzled it down.

I looked at Tony. 'Perhaps she doesn't need a check up, after all.'

Tony was on the phone when I got in from waving the girls off to school.

'Yes. They were outside, in the grounds of the animal centre when we got up. Yes, the gate was closed and padlocked. It's about four feet high, so no, I doubt very much that they could have jumped over – certainly not the St Bernard anyway. Someone must have dropped them over it, but the big one – Christ knows how they got that over the top. Yes, they're both in good, bodily condition – coats are good, and the St Bernard has been well groomed, from what I can see.'

I'd gone to see the two dogs after I'd said goodbye to the girls, and when I spoke to them, they both stood up at the wire and wagged their tails at me, and there was no sign of the aggression they'd shown earlier.

It was my day off, so when Anna arrived, I explained what had happened.

'They must have been dumped,' she responded. 'They couldn't have got in on their own, and anyway, where would they have come from? We're in the middle of nowhere, and I know for a fact that the nearest neighbour has Jack Russells, so they don't belong to her.'

'That's what we thought too. Oh, I don't know, it's all very strange.'

'People are strange – look at us for a start.' She laughed. 'Christ knows where I'm going to put them though, we're already overflowing with dogs. Any suggestions?'

I thought for a moment. 'I'd put them in the covered run and stick a couple of beds in there. They aren't going to fit into one kennel together, and I don't think we should separate them. Just have to hope that Tom doesn't turn up with any strays today …'

'Hmm, good idea, I'll do that. Anyway, it's your day off, and you've already had a bad start.' Anna got my arm and pulled me towards the door. 'What are you up to – anything nice?' she asked, as she shoved me out.

'I'm going to walk the dogs, write a letter to my sister, meet Tony for lunch somewhere, and then have a nice, quiet couple of hours reading before the girls get home from school.'

'You go and have fun. See you later.' She waved and shut the door on me.

The dogs knew we were nearly at the woods, and started leaping around and panting in excitement, and as I turned the last corner, Tina stood on the seat behind me, and barked into my right ear. By the time I'd switched off the engine they'd all joined Tina and the noise was deafening. I gathered up their leads, opened the van door and laughed as they all fell over each other to get out – except for my old girl Tuppy, who waited until I picked her up.

I watched as they disappeared into the trees.

After an hour of running around at break-neck speed, they panted their way back to the van and collapsed on the seats.

A letter to my sister was long overdue, so armed with a biro and a mug of tea, I sat down and wrote six pages. I'd even bought a stamp to post it with, and as soon as I'd finished, I walked out of my front gate, towards the post box.

I rarely had time to admire my surroundings, but as I walked along, I noticed red and orange berries in the hedge-row, and thought immediately of Christmas. Huge black-berries begged to be picked, so I stopped and indulged myself, and decided to bring the girls along the lane after school to pick some. They loved helping my mum cook, and would enjoy making a blackberry pie.

Back at my gate, I stopped to admire a purple flower, and as I bent down to see if it had a nice smell, noticed a very damp, cardboard box in the long grass. I didn't like litter, so went to pick it up, but it was heavier than I expected it to be. Alarm bells rang in my head, and I ripped the top of the box open.

Two ginger kittens lay, side by side, on a soggy blanket, in the bottom of the box. I gasped, and picked one of them up. It was alive, but very cold, and not very strong, and its eyes were caked in crusty green muck, so it couldn't open them. It was breathing through its mouth, as its nose was completely bunged up with dry snot. A look at the other kitten showed it was slightly bigger, but in the same state.

With them both stuck up under my jumper, I left the box and rushed round to Anna.

'Look; look at these poor little things.' I showed her what I'd found.

'Oh my.' She was horrified. 'Where did you find them? Let's get the kettle on and get some warm milk into them.' We went to the kitchen and I told her.

She held one of them to her, to warm it up, and as she got the milk ready, I smothered their caked eyes and noses in Vaseline, to try and soften the muck before pulling it off, fearing their skin would come off with it.

I held them while Anna syringed rehydration fluid into them, but they struggled to drink it because they couldn't breathe. We did get some into them, but nowhere near enough, so I got a cotton wool ball, and gently wiped the dried snot away. One clear nostril was enough to make a difference, so I passed the kitten that was half done to Anna, and she syringed a drop of milk into its mouth. It liked the milk, and swallowed.

I cleaned one nostril on the second kitten, and passed that one to Anna, who had been able to get quite a bit of milk into the first one, but just as she started feeding it, the phone rang.

'Oh … go away,' she said, not wanting to have to answer it.

'Leave it,' I barked. 'This is more important; they can ring back.'

We carried on cleaning and feeding the kittens.

'I've been trying to ring you, on the phone indoors as well as the one out here.' Tony stood in the office doorway. 'We were supposed to be having lunch.'

'Oh God – I'm sorry.' I got up and gave him a kiss. 'I found these by our front gate.' I went to a cardboard cat carrier, and pulled open a crocheted blanket that had been knitted, specially for the cats, by a little old lady.

Tony looked at the kittens. 'By our front gate? That was lucky then, wasn't it – how often do we use that?'

'I know. I think they must have been there for more than a day, because they're quite weak, and the box is very damp. It's still there actually.'

'Whereabouts? I want to take some photos of it. I'll also give HQ a call – and the local papers, see if we can find who did it. Why the bloody hell did they feel the need to just dump them at the gate …?' He reached down and stroked one of them, before marching out of the door, seething.

He took his photos, called HQ and the local paper … 'Look at the time.' He showed me his watch. 'So much for having lunch out. Shall we make do with a sandwich?'

'Yes, I already thought that. I'll go and see what there is.' I went over to my kitchen and made him a ham sandwich.

He winked at me as I handed him the plate. 'Thank you darling.'

'Right,' I said to him and Anna. 'Since the kittens are looking a bit better already, and the vet does his weekly visit today, and as lunch is off, and the girls will be home in about an hour, I'm going to go and curl up with a good book.' I smiled and waved.

My hour went far too quickly, and before I knew it, the girls were home from school.

'As soon as you've changed your uniforms, we're going blackberry picking, and when Grandma's over tomorrow, you can help her make a blackberry pie.' They rushed off to change, and armed with a plastic tub each, we went off down the lane.

It was Lisa who, on our way back home, first heard the shouting. 'Mummy, can you hear someone shouting?'

I stopped and listened. Yes – I could hear Anna shouting. 'Quick – come on.' I grabbed Edwina's hand and walked as fast as possible back to the centre.

'DON'T YOU DARE CALL ME AN AWKWARD COW … I'M NOT BEING AWKWARD … WE DON'T HAVE ANY ROOM.'

'Go indoors,' I ordered the girls, and went over to Anna. 'What's going on?'

Anna turned to me. 'This … gentleman, is expecting me to take in this dog.' She pointed to a liver and white Springer Spaniel. 'I've explained that we don't have any room, and that we are already overcrowded at the moment. I've suggested that we put the dog on the waiting list, as we are having to do with other dogs, and told the … gentleman, that we will get the dog in as soon as we can. But HE won't have it, and has called me an awkward cow – twice.'

Anna was bright red. I'd never seen her like this before.

'Right.' I looked at the man. 'If Anna has explained our current situation to you already, there's little that I can add.'

'Are you a stupid cow then?' he spat at me.

I noticed his teeth were black, where they met the gums.

'I don't want this dog.' He kicked at the dog, but it moved out of his way. 'How many times do I have to tell you – you bloody morons. I don't care whether you've got room or not, I DON'T WANT THIS DOG.'

'Don't you call us morons, it's you that doesn't get it,' Anna retaliated. 'We don't have any room, so we cannot take the dog.'

I glared at him. 'Yes, occasionally I believe I am a stupid cow. I must be, to be standing here listening to you being so rude. Come on, Anna, it's pointless, he's not listening.'

I walked away, and up the drive, towards the office, hoping that Anna would follow. I heaved a sigh of relief when she stomped past me.

'Okay, have it your own way, you silly bitches. I'm going now – to take him up onto the A27, where I'm going to chuck him out of my car and to hell with him.'

We stopped, and turned round abruptly. Anna marched back down towards him, so I followed.

'Come here, you git.' The Spaniel dodged him for a second or two, but then he grabbed it by a back leg, and hauled it into the air. It yelped as he held it, suspended, while he opened up the boot of his car.

He threw it, with some force, into the boot, and slammed it shut.

'Be seeing you.' His face contorted into an ugly leer, as he started the engine.

You bastard … I grabbed the gate and pulled it open enough to get through. He wasn't leaving with that dog.

'That dog is not going anywhere in the boot of your car!' screamed Anna, as she ripped the keys out of the ignition.

Like lightning, she had the boot open, and the dog in her arms. She threw his keys on the ground.

'BASTARD!' She ran in through the gate.

I closed the gate behind her. 'Piss off.' I gave him the most evil glare I could muster. 'Go on, just piss off.'

'Aw … She just saved the little doggy's life.' He revved really hard, and drove off.

'You okay?' I looked over the bottom part of the stable door into the office. Anna was crying.

I opened the door carefully, as the Spaniel was loose in there with her. It came to me, tail between its legs, almost crawling on its belly. I bent down and stroked it.

'What a bastard,' she almost whispered, as she wiped her eyes with her sleeve.

'I know. Cigarette?' I offered her my packet, and lit the one she took.

The dog rolled over onto its back, and lay there. 'Well, at least we know that you're a boy, and you haven't been castrated yet.' I flicked the ash off the end of my cigarette, and looked at Anna. 'You were brilliant out there.'

'Ha … no. I wasn't brilliant. I lost my temper, which is something I hate doing. I went down to his level, and I was unprofessional. I swore at him.' She pulled on the cigarette.

'I swore at him too. He would have done it; I know he would have done it. He told me that you'd saved the dog's life, and you know what? I actually believe him.'

'Did he say that? Oh my God – what a shit.'

'Yes, Anna, what a shit. Marie would have been very proud of you.'

Anna smiled. 'Yes, she would, wouldn't she. Good job she wasn't here; I think she'd have killed him.' We giggled at the thought of how Marie would have dealt with him, and dealt with him she would, probably in much the same way that her mother had.

Now we had to make room for the Spaniel.

An elderly stray had been in the kennels for the full seven days, and as no-one had claimed him, he'd been signed over by Tom, and was being put up for re-homing the next day. He was a lovely old boy, and very good with other dogs, so we put him in with Judy, a twelve-year-old bitch whose owner had recently died.

'I have a name for the old boy,' said Anna, as she put his bed in the kennel, next to Judy's.

'What's that?'

'Punch.'

We burst out laughing. Impulsively, I hugged Anna, and she smiled; everything was all right again.

I was sitting indoors, watching the telly, when the phone rang.

'Hi Mum. Yes, we went and picked some blackberries, and they can't wait to make a pie with you tomorrow. Yes, we've got some apples on the trees here if you want some. How was my quiet day off? Oh, nothing much happened … not really.'

CHAPTER 18

Fate?

Mother and daughter smiled up at me, from two separate photos on the front page of the local newspaper. Anna was holding the two ginger kittens that had been dumped in the cardboard box, and Marie was kneeling between the St Bernard and the German Shepherd. The photos dominated the page, along with the headline:

'DO YOU RECOGNISE THESE ANIMALS?'

A lengthy and detailed story followed.

'Wow – that's a brilliant article.' I smiled at Tony. 'Different animals being dumped by different people on the same day certainly got their attention.' I showed him the front page of the newspaper I'd driven into town for early that morning.

'I must admit I'm very pleased, I think they've done an excellent job. Now, we just need to wait and see what comes from it all.'

Within a few minutes, it was obvious what was going to come from it. The phone rang, but as we were closed, it went onto the answering machine. Then the phone rang again, and again …

'The phone hasn't stopped ringing, has it?' I sighed to Anna at tea break that morning. 'You know what's going to happen – we're going to spend the day answering it, and not get all the cleaning done. Not that I'm complaining, because it would be great if someone did tell us who owned them all, but somehow, I don't think we'll be that lucky.'

At eleven o'clock, I switched off the answering machine. The phone rang immediately.

'HELLO,' a male voice shouted down the phone at me.

'Hello, RSPCA, Jane speaking, can I help you?'

'YES. I WANT TO SPEAK TO THE INSPECTOR.'

'He's not here at the moment, can I take a message?'

'CAN YOU GET HIM TO PHONE ME? I KNOW THOSE DOGS.'

I raised my eyebrows to Anna. 'You know the dogs? Great, can I take your phone number please.'

He gave me his number.

The first phone call I'd taken – and already someone claimed to know the dogs. I couldn't wait for Tony to get back.

'TONY'S HERE,' Anna called up to the top dog run, where I was shovelling up poo. I rushed down to tell him.

'We've had so many calls about the dogs!' I said, as I hugged him.

'Good. HQ have had a few as well.'

Anna passed him a coffee. 'The owners were mad to do what they did. They obviously didn't bargain on a big front page spread about them being dumped here.'

'Thank you.' He smiled at her. 'I think you're right. And hopefully it will send a message to anyone else who might be thinking about dumping their animals: don't.'

'Precisely.' I nodded in agreement.

'So, if you've had that many calls, you probably know their names then.' He looked at both of us.

'Pippa and Muppet,' said Anna through her lips as she lit a cigarette.

'Both are spayed bitches,' I added.

'Both are about four years old,' said Anna.

'Both lovely with people,' I continued.

'Both bad with dogs.' Anna laughed.

'We know that, don't we?' I grinned at Tony.

'Not much I can tell you then.' He looked at the armchair, then at Anna, before sitting down quickly. 'I'll get in while your dogs are out.'

'So what next then?' I asked, as Tony dunked a digestive biscuit into his coffee.

He just managed to get his hand under the biscuit before the soggy bit dropped off. 'I'm not sure. One of the people that phoned HQ said it's all very sad. The dogs had always been well loved and looked after. Apparently the man who'd owned them told everyone they'd gone to a good home.' He slurped his coffee-logged biscuit out of his hand.

'Well they had,' said Anna. 'This is a good home; a very good animal home.'

I laughed. 'Mmm, very quick – I like it. But why did he do it?' I looked at Tony. 'Why did he need to get rid of them?'

'Apparently his wife is ill, and the dogs weren't getting the care they needed.'

'Oh, my heart is bleeding,' I said, sarcastically. 'Loads of people get ill, but they don't all dump their dogs over the gate of RSPCA animal centres because of it, do they?'

Tony took a chocolate bourbon out of the packet. 'I agree, entirely. I've got his address, and will be off shortly to pay him a visit.'

I giggled as he pulled the biscuit out of his coffee, and two thirds of it broke off, and plopped back in.

The day continued, with call after call about the dogs, including many offers of homes for them both. No-one phoned about the kittens.

That evening, I leaned my elbows across Tony's back as he sat, bent over his desk, writing. 'Are you going to come and eat? It's nearly half past nine, and you've been sitting here writing for over three hours.'

He took his glasses off and rubbed his eyes. 'Yes, sorry. I just wanted to get this finished.'

I rested my head on top of his. 'I didn't expect myself to say this, but it is a sad story about the dogs, isn't it?'

Tony had visited the owners of the dogs that afternoon, and the man had apologised as soon as he'd opened the door. The wife was ill; very ill, and it was obvious from the start that she had no idea of what he'd done. Tony said nothing when her husband told her that he'd knocked on the door of the wrong house. Instead, he arranged to meet up with the man, away from the house, later in the afternoon.

The man said he'd dropped the dogs over the gate out of desperation, but immediately regretted his decision. He'd tried, very quietly, to get the dogs back again, but they'd gone off sniffing everywhere, and then suddenly there were other dogs running around, so he'd panicked and driven off.

He'd done it because he'd just had to give up his job to look after his sick wife, and money was very tight. He was struggling already, financially, and the dogs were expensive to feed. The reason he dumped them, was because he knew he wouldn't be able to walk into the centre, and say he didn't want them any more; he was a coward, and knew he'd cry.

Tony put his arms up around my neck. 'We're so lucky.' He turned his head sideways and kissed my cheek.

'Why?'

'Look at us; we have our health, our jobs, and each other. He's got a sick wife, no job, and little money.'

I hugged Tony tight. 'What now?' I said quietly.

He swivelled his chair round, took my hands in his and looked at me. 'I'm not going to take it any further.'

'Good. I'm glad.' I bent forward and kissed him.

'He shouldn't have done it – we all know that, but he didn't do it for malicious reasons. He loved those dogs very much … and was in such a state when I spoke to him.' Tony put his head down and went quiet.

'I think you've made the right decision. You won't achieve anything by taking the matter any further, and I, for one, am very pleased. Sometimes humans need a bit of compassion, too, Tony – but only sometimes.' I smiled as I pulled his hand. 'Come and eat.'

He sat down at the table, but only picked at his meal.

'Good morning!' Anna flung open the gate with gusto. Her dogs leapt about in the back of her estate, wagging their tails and barking in excitement. 'I have a wonderful home for the two ginger kittens!' she shouted, as she reversed up the driveway. 'And the people are prepared to wait for as long as necessary until they have them.'

I pulled the gate closed again and shouted back. 'Who's that then?'

'A couple I've known for years. They've got two cats already, and said only recently that they were thinking of getting two more. They live in the country, on a very quiet road, and although they've only got a small garden, it backs onto woods and a little stream. I reckon the kittens would love it there. They've got a cat flap in the back door, and the cats can come and go as they please. The cats they've already got sleep on the bed with them, and get the most expensive tinned food to eat.'

'Sounds very nice, Anna. And they don't mind waiting to see whether we find the owner? Because if Tony does find out who dumped them, he will try and prosecute. The kittens would probably have died in that cardboard box if I hadn't gone to post a letter that day.'

Anna opened the office door and stood still as her dogs barged in past her. 'I've explained everything to them and as long as they can come up here and get to know the kittens while they wait, they really don't mind.'

'Well, that's them sorted then.' I followed her into the office. 'I'm sure it will be sooner rather than later, as we haven't had a single call from anyone about them.'

'Frustrating, isn't it?' she responded. 'All those calls about the dogs, and nothing about the kittens. But at least they're alive, and they'll have such a good home with these people.'

'Yep, you're right – at least they're alive.' I nodded as my mind went back to the soggy cardboard box. 'You might as well tell Tony they've already got a home, and ask him how long he wants to give it before we let the couple adopt them.'

Anna headed off to the cattery, I opened up the kennel blocks, and we began the daily task of cleaning.

'The St Bernard and the German Shepherd are signed over to us now, and can be re-homed,' Tony said, that lunchtime.

'Well we've had loads of calls from people willing to adopt them,' I replied. 'The one I think would be most suitable is a builder who owns his own business and has always taken his dogs to work with him. He's just lost a St Bernard, and had a Shepherd before that. Most of the other offers are for one or the other dog, not both of them. It would be better for them to stay together, so I'd rather go for him. He's married, and has two teenage kids who love dogs. In fact it was one of the kids who first saw the article in the paper, and begged him to ring us.'

'Has he been and seen the dogs?'

'Oh yes. He brought the wife and kids too, and they all fell in love with them.'

'Okay. Can you phone him and arrange a home-check? I'd like to go myself, under the circumstances.'

'Will do.' I smiled at Tony. 'Hopefully that's the dogs re-homed, as well as the kittens.'

The next morning, two very eager teenagers waited outside the gate with their father to adopt their new dogs.

Adoption forms completed, the family made their way back to their car, where the St Bernard jumped up, put her giant paws on the shoulders of the boy, and slobbered all over his face before jumping onto the seat. The Shepherd was a little more reserved, but wagged her tail as she climbed slowly into the back of the car with the girl. The man beamed happily and waved goodbye to us. We stood and watched until the car disappeared.

Tony sighed. 'Nice family.'

'Yes, they are. And I'm sure they'll all be very happy.' I looked at him. 'Are you going to tell the owner, I mean, the one that put them over the gate?'

'I'd like him to know they've gone to a good home – yes. I think it'll make him feel a bit better. Obviously he won't know where, but I will call him and tell him.'

'I'm glad. I think he'd like to know.' I linked my arm in his as we walked back inside.

Three days later, having heard nothing about the ginger kittens, I stood with Anna and waved as they went off with their new owners too. 'Oh well, another good home for another two animals.' I wiped my eyes. 'I still find it hard to believe that they could have died in that bloody box if I hadn't had a letter to post.'

'Fate,' she replied with a smile. 'You were meant to find them.'

'Fate! Do you seriously believe in that stuff?' I laughed at the thought. 'Well I wish "fate" would find someone to adopt the Springer Spaniel you grabbed out of the boot. He's a pedigree, he's gorgeous, he's young, he's good with all the animals, and he's still homeless.'

'Ooo – you non-believer you!' Anna retaliated. 'Yes – I do believe in that stuff!'

'I wish I had your faith, woman.' I grinned at her. 'But I don't.'

'You mark my words – fate plays a big part in everything,' she insisted.

We agreed to disagree, and went to feed the animals their evening meal.

The next morning, a car was already parked outside the gate when Anna went to open up.

'Someone's keen,' she said, raising her eyebrows as she walked back into the office.

A minute later, a man poked his head round the door. 'Morning.' He smiled at us.

We answered in unison, smiling back at him.

As she closed the door, Anna continued, 'Can I help you?'

'I do hope so. I've been told there's a Springer Spaniel here, is that right?'

Anna and I looked at each other before she replied. 'Yes. Yes, that's right, there is. A male, but we don't know how old, although the vet has estimated that he's only about a year or so. We've had him castrated, so all we'd need to do is carry out a home-check. Would you like to have a look at him?'

'Oh yes please,' he replied, eagerly.

Anna got the dog out and the man took him for a walk round the centre.

'Fingers crossed!' she whispered to me. 'He seems very nice, and he's got a Springer bitch already. He wants to go and get his dog and bring her along later to see how they get on.'

She stopped as the man made his way back over towards us.

'He's a lovely boy.' He patted the dog's head. 'I'd like to go and get my wife, and my dog, if that's okay. They both need to approve, or I'll be in trouble.' He laughed.

'Oh, that's no problem, and there's no rush either.' Anna had already got a new card from the drawer. 'I'll put this card up saying that he has someone interested in him, and is no longer available for homing.' She gave him a huge smile. 'See you later then.'

At three-thirty, a pretty little Spaniel accompanied its owners up the driveway.

'Hello! I've brought the boss to come and see the Spaniel.' He pointed to the dog, whose half tail wagged so quickly it was hard to see. 'And my wife, who is much easier to please.' She smiled as he introduced her.

Anna went and got the dog.

After much leaping about on the end of the lead, and a bit of snapping, the bitch decided she liked him, and rushed around him in a demented fashion.

The male was somewhat overwhelmed by it all, but wagged his half tail almost as fast as she wagged hers.

Anna left them alone to have a chat about the dog. She showed me her fingers, which were crossed on both hands.

'We've made a decision.' The man beamed at us. 'We'd like to offer him a home.'

Anna jumped up and grabbed the writing pad. 'Oh that's good! Right. I'll just take down your details, and arrange a home-check. It should only take a day or two, and then you can come and collect him. What's your address?'

They both told her.

'Wait a minute.' She stopped and looked at them.

I suddenly got a bad feeling.

'I know where that is,' she continued.

'Yes,' smiled the man. 'We live next to the people who've just adopted the ginger kittens.'

My bad feeling disappeared.

'Oh my God!' said Anna, and laughed.

'They asked us to say hello, and tell you the kittens are doing well,' he continued. 'It was them that told us about the dog.'

Anna knew the house, and the garden, so we agreed there was no need for a home-check, and they could take him whenever they were ready. They took him then.

Anna and I stood next to each other in the kitchen, mixing up the dog biscuit with the tinned meat.

I vigorously scraped out the remains from a tin, and plopped it into the bowl. 'Before you say anything – I know.'

She grinned at me. 'Say it then.'

I stopped scraping, and looked at her, before saying, very seriously, 'It was fate.'

She smiled at me. 'Yep – it was fate.'

We carried on mixing up the dog food.

CHAPTER 19

The Dog Show with a Difference

'WE RECEIVE NO STATE AID.'

I studied one of the new RSPCA leaflets that had been sent to us by HQ to put on display. Accompanying the bold statement was a picture of a young-looking dog, head cocked sideways as it stared out solemnly from behind the bars of its kennel.

Many RSPCA animal centres throughout the country were run by individual committees, but came under the auspices of RSPCA HQ, and like us, they all needed money, but none received state aid. A lot of people believed that the 'royal' prefix meant we were funded by the government in some way, but we most definitely weren't.

One way of making money was to board animals while the owners were away on holiday, and we had a block of four boarding kennels, and one of four cat units, built specifically for this purpose.

We had the contract with the local council to accommodate stray dogs brought in by Tom, the dog warden, and we made a small profit from goods we sold in our shop.

Over the previous year we'd held several jumble sale/barbecues, with each raising a good amount of money, and we also charged an adoption fee for each animal.

We received donations from members of the public; some large, mostly small, which helped immensely, but even with all of these things combined, there was never enough, and we faced a constant struggle to make ends meet.

Most of the dogs and cats needed neutering before being re-homed, and those that were already neutered still had to be checked by the vet to make sure they were healthy before they left us. Animal food, staff wages, heating for the kennels and cattery and maintenance of the buildings all took their toll on the finances.

We had to do more.

'Any suggestions, Anna?'

She looked thoughtful. 'Hmm, now let me think.' She reached across the table for her cigarette packet.

I sighed. 'I know that whatever we do will only be a drop in the ocean, but all the jumble sales added together made a good amount of money, didn't they? So if we can do something else on a regular basis, we may be able to make another reasonable amount throughout the year.' I rested my chin on the palm of my hand. 'Oh … I've thought and thought, but I'm bloody useless at coming up with ideas.'

Anna puffed her cigarette into life before answering. 'We could do a dog show, but it probably wouldn't make much money.'

I sat up. 'A dog show. Yes.' I conjured up an image in my mind. 'I like it.'

'It would only need to be a fun thing – you know, not your serious classes, just waggiest tail, and dog who looks most like its owner …' Anna looked at her own dogs, slumped on top of each other on the armchair. 'Which one of mine looks most like me?'

I laughed. All of Anna's dogs were black and white – she had very brown hair. All of her dogs were plump – she was slim. 'The only thing you've all got in common is short hair.'

'I'll give that class a miss then.' She giggled. 'We could have best Irish brace.'

I creased my eyebrows. 'What is an Irish brace?'

'Two dogs who live together but are completely different, like … oooh, a Great Dane and a Chihuahua. Don't ask me why it's called that because I haven't got a clue, but it's surprising how many people have such different breeds together. We had a dog show here a few years ago, and it was great fun. Loads of people came.'

'Right – that's it, then; a dog show it is.' I was pleased. 'We can make sandwiches to sell, and refreshments, which will all make money. We'll need to get plenty of advertising done; I want this to be a real success.'

'How about a raffle, too?' Anna continued. 'We could try and get some bits from shops and businesses to give as prizes.'

'Even better. You know, Anna – this could turn out to be a good money spinner, as well as a lot of fun.'

Anna grinned at me. 'Do you want me to ask Patty to help? I don't think she's done a dog show before, but I'm sure she'd enjoy organising one, just as much as she enjoys doing the jumble sales.'

'That would be great – if she doesn't mind. I do feel like we take advantage of her though.'

'She doesn't mind a bit. Since her husband died she's been very lonely, so this gives her something worthwhile to think about, and do. Leave it with me.' Anna winked.

As usual, Patty was pleased to help, and had very quickly arranged her group of women to make sandwiches, sausage rolls and cakes. She also contacted local shops and businesses, and managed to persuade most of them to part with something, then spent hours trundling around, collecting all the donated items. Before long the jumble shed was stacked with over twenty raffle prizes.

'Wow,' said Anna, as we stared at the growing mountain of goods. 'Can you believe this lot? There's a TV here, for goodness' sake!' She picked up an envelope and pulled out a card. 'And a voucher for a weekend in this posh hotel! Patty really went for it, didn't she?'

'She certainly did.' I struggled to pick up a huge bottle of whisky that had been donated by the off licence in town. 'Look at this, Anna; it must be worth a small fortune. I think we should get posters out everywhere, with a list of the raffle prizes on them. That'd encourage even more people hopefully. My dad would come just to try and win the whisky! I'll ask Tony to do the posters on his computer to make them look as professional as possible.'

With my head full of ideas for the posters, I went off to clean out the rabbits.

Tony enjoyed designing things, and with the new art program he'd recently bought for his computer, he was well away. I joined him once the girls were in bed, and made my suggestions, and at two fifteen in the middle of that night, we both sat back and stared at the end result.

I stretched and yawned. 'That is pretty darn good.'

Tony yawned too. 'It's not bad, is it?' He stood up and pushed his swivel chair back with his legs. 'I'll just print one now so we can see what it looks like properly, and then I'll do the rest in the morning.'

I looked at my watch and groaned. 'It is the morning. Oh God – I didn't realise how long we'd been doing it.' I yawned again as the printer zipped into action.

There was so much on the poster that it took a while to print, and we watched in silence as our efforts slowly emerged on paper.

'Hmm.' Tony muttered to himself as he looked at the finished product.

'What's wrong?'

'I don't like the writing now. I should have used Times New Roman after all; it's easy to read, unlike that.' He pointed at the print which was quite swirly and fancy. 'I'll change it tomorrow.'

'Well I think it's really good and you should leave it as it is. It's already taken what … five and a half hours to do?' He yawned again as I looked at him.

'No. I don't like it. It won't take long to change.' He turned off the computer. 'Come on, let's go to bed.'

There was no sign of Tony when my alarm went off four and a half hours later, but I knew where I'd find him.

'How long have you been sitting here?' I kissed the top of his head and looked at the poster which had now been changed.

'Not long,' he replied. The skin on the top of his un-drunk coffee said otherwise.

I felt the side of the mug. 'Long enough for this to go completely cold.' I picked up the new poster. 'Are you satisfied with this one then?'

He smiled. 'I think so.'

'Good.' I put it back on the desk, then picked it up again and had a closer look. I'd just realised that not a single one of my ideas had been used.

The posters were out in shop windows, the last raffle prize had been collected. The bread, sausage meat and pastry had been bought, and was sitting in Patty's freezer, and the vet had agreed to be the dog show judge. A meeting had been held, and all the volunteers attended to decide who was doing what. We were ready.

On the morning of the dog show, I pulled back the bedroom curtains and looked out at the sun, rising into the perfectly clear, pale blue sky. I smiled to myself; this was the weather I'd prayed for. Excitement welled up inside me as I anticipated the day ahead.

Patty arrived early, and began by setting up the raffle prizes on two tables next to the summer house. She sat a very large teddy bear on a blanket on the ground between the tables, and stood the whisky bottle in front of it. A red bow tied its left paw to the bottle.

By mid-morning, nine volunteers had transformed the animal centre. Opposite the raffle prizes, another table was adorned with red, blue, green, and yellow rosettes, and three small, silver trophies stood proud among them. I picked one up and examined it. Engraved across the front of it was: Dog the Judge Would Most Like to Take Home. I looked around for Patty, who was engrossed in laying out trays full of sausage rolls. She must have paid for the trophies and the engraving herself, as we had only paid for the rosettes. I thought once again how lucky we were to have her.

Paper plates piled with sandwiches covered three tables, and next to them stood the tea urn that had recently been given to us. I loved it, as it was so much easier than constantly boiling a kettle. Then my mouth watered as I came across butterfly cakes, fairy cakes, madeleines and nameless sponges nestling against each other on two more tables.

A banging noise made me turn to see what was happening, and there was Marie, bashing a wooden stake into the ground. An area of about thirty feet square had been marked out with more stakes and a piece of rope; the beginnings of the ring for the dog show. I beamed. It was almost time.

The vet arrived, and made straight for the sausage rolls. He said he was starving, having missed out on breakfast due to performing an emergency Caesarean section on a dog. I saw him hand over a five pound note for them. The volunteer shook her head and waved her hands at him, but he insisted, and dropped it into the money pot. He was gruff sometimes, but had a heart of gold.

'How are you doing?' said Anna, when she found me in the kitchen.

'The kennels are done and I've had most of the dogs out for a walk around. How about you?'

'All finished. The cats were pretty clean today. I fed and watered the rabbits and guinea pigs but didn't clean out any hutches; they can be done tomorrow.' She got herself a mug from the cupboard.

'Good, we're doing okay then. I'm just going to have a quick cuppa then I'll walk the rest of the dogs. Is Mr Ying shut in yet?' Mr Ying was a Chinese goose who enjoyed pecking people, particularly men. He was a permanent resident at the centre, and as a rule roamed freely with his two female companions, but when we held an event it was safer to shut him in the goat paddock shelter for the day.

'He's already in.' She poured milk into both mugs. 'So – shall I help you with the last few dogs?'

'If you don't mind, that'd be great, thanks.' I added the sugar.

'It's looking good out there.' Anna continued as she poured in the boiling water. 'Mind, the vet has made a dent in the food already – he hasn't stopped eating since he got here.'

'I did notice. God – I wish I could eat like that and still be as thin as he is.' Since marrying Tony, I'd put on several pounds due to eating large quantities of chocolate whilst lying in bed, reading.

'Worms,' said Anna.

'What?' I replied.

'Worms; he could have worms.'

I snorted and shoved her through the kitchen doorway. 'Anna!'

We stood together outside the back of the dog runs, having a quiet cigarette before the fun began, and looked down the road at the lengthening queue of people. Dogs of all shapes and sizes stood with their owners; some patiently, some noisily, and some sniffing the bums of others who really didn't want their bums to be sniffed. Including some owners …

As I looked along the queue, I felt a swell of emotion inside me. I was always humbled at the thought that we arranged an event and people came in their droves to support the animals.

At two o'clock, Marie opened the gate, and then stood in the middle of the driveway, rattling a bucket in each hand as she offered to release people of the burden of carrying around all that change.

Anna looked at me. 'Can you hear her? She's a cheeky little cow, isn't she?'

I laughed. 'Yes she is, but look at the response she's getting – people obviously love it; they're laughing and chucking loads in the buckets.'

As if Marie knew we were watching her, she turned, and lifted both buckets to us. We smiled and waved back at her.

Anna looked at me. 'Come on then woman, we've got a dog show to do.'

'Yep.' I smiled, as she squeezed my arm. She knew I was always a bit nervous about how things would go. 'Come on then – let's do it.'

I adjusted my navy blue RSPCA dungarees, straightened my RSPCA name badge, and proudly walked over to the people queuing to enter the first class. Both Anna and myself were going to spend the afternoon mingling, as we wanted to be free to talk to anyone interested in adopting one of the unwanted animals in our care.

The first class to be held – Dog That Looked Most Like its Owner – was won by an Afghan hound, because the owner, whose hair was almost the same soft brown colour as the dog's, had had her hair cut to about the same length as the dog's fur. The resemblance was uncanny.

A Dachshund caused a bit of a kerfuffle in the Irish Brace class, by refusing to parade around the ring. Instead, it lay down and wouldn't move. Its companion, a Beagle, sat down next to it and leaned against its back. The lady owner called and cajoled, but the pair seemed to have gone deaf. The vet encouraged the owners of the other entrants to continue by walking around them, but an Irish Wolfhound appeared not to be too bothered and walked over them both instead. The Jack Russell accompanying the huge dog yapped and snapped as it passed. The Beagle stood up and stiffened, with the short hairs on the scruff of its neck rising, but the Dachshund didn't move.

The vet decided to take action, and carefully picked up the sausage dog. He chatted with the grateful owner before putting the dog down at the end of the row. It lay down again, and the Beagle leaned against it.

After much deliberation, and a quick chat with his wife, who had only just arrived, the vet chose the Irish Wolfhound and Jack Russell as the winners, and amid much applause, he presented the beaming owner of the two dogs with rosettes. As the rest of the dogs and owners filed out of the ring, the Dachshund still laid where the vet had put it earlier, and the owner still called and cajoled. I felt for her, as my dogs were often disobedient, and went and picked up the dog.

'That was rather embarrassing,' the elderly lady said, as I put the dog down on the ground.

'Oh, don't worry. I think everyone enjoyed it. He's got character.' I stroked the unwilling dog on his head.

'Thank you, dear,' she responded. 'I think you're being generous, though. It's called stubbornness really, not character. If he had a little finger, I'm quite sure I would be considered as being wrapped around it.'

I laughed at the way she put it, and admitted that I owned dogs with the same stubbornness. The Dachshund had decided it was time to move, and with surprising agility, took off towards the refreshments.

'Goodbye dear, and thank you again,' the owner called over her shoulder as she was pulled along.

'Goodbye,' I called back.

The Dog with the Waggiest Tail class was already underway as I went back to the ring. The vet appeared to be in his element, slapping his legs, leaping about, whistling, getting on his knees and pawing at the ground and woofing, all to a dog which wasn't wagging its tail. The dog, which looked like a Bloodhound cross, had the most serious expression across its face as it watched the vet's antics, but the crowd were in hysterics. I joined in the laughter, and knew that people would remember this dog show for the vet, if nothing else. I'd remember it for the same reason, as I never dreamed I'd see him behaving like that.

The owner of the serious dog laughed as much as the rest of us, and also tried to make the dog wag its tail by scratching its back, and behind its ears. She joined the vet, slapping her legs as she called to him, telling the dog what a good boy he was, and even giving him a treat. He took and ate the titbit, but his tail didn't move. The vet moved on along the row of dogs, all wagging their tails, but without doubt the waggiest belonged to a Spaniel cross with only half a tail, which moved so quickly it was difficult to watch.

The vet finally went back to the serious dog, but all further attempts he made to make him wag his tail failed dismally, and with a smile and a bow to the owner, the vet gave in.

He walked into the centre of the ring and held his hand up for attention. 'THE DOG WITH THE WAGGIEST TAIL IS … THE SPRINGER SPANIEL CROSS!'

Cheers for the Spaniel erupted, and the owner ran with the dog into the middle, where the vet presented her with her rosette. She pinned it straight onto the dog's collar, and his half-tail wagged ecstatically as he jumped up at her. The vet applauded, and the ring slowly emptied.

There was a half an hour break before the next class, so everyone dispersed. I went to find Anna.

'All okay?' I asked her.

'Brilliant! I've just been over to the raffle table, and they're really pleased with the number of tickets they've sold.'

'Do you think we should ask the vet to shout to everyone as soon as the dog show bit is finished, to say that if anyone wants to buy tickets, the raffle's going to be drawn within the next, I don't know – fifteen minutes?' I looked at Anna expectantly.

'Yes, good idea. I'm sure he won't mind after seeing the way he's thrown himself into everything this afternoon.'

'That's just what I thought. He's really good at getting people to listen to him. I'll go and ask him before he starts the next class. See you later then.' I left Anna, and walked towards the refreshments table to get a cup of tea.

Vicious growling and snarling suddenly erupted next to the summer house, and by the time I got there, a full-blown dog fight was underway. A Labrador and a Border Collie rolled around on the grass, their leads getting more and more tangled, their teenage owners getting more and more frantic. The boy yanked on the lead but lost his grip on it, and the girl shrieked at her dog, whichever one it was. Blood mixed with saliva in the mouth of the Collie, and as it hung onto the neck of the Labrador, that dog's golden coat became pink.

I was well adept at pulling fighting dogs apart, thanks to Tony's April and my Tina, and so plunged into the scuffle without a second thought. The dog nearest to me was the Collie, so I grabbed it by its check chain with my left hand, saving my stronger, right hand for the Labrador, which I grabbed by the collar. Once they felt my grip, they both stopped, which made separating them much easier. The Labrador looked up at me and straight away wagged his tail. The Border Collie had one last snap, before turning to the young girl.

'Here you go. No real harm done.' I smiled at the girl, who looked as if she was about to cry.

The boy stepped forward and picked up the end of the Labrador's lead. 'Thank you,' he said, shyly.

'David? David! What's going on? Someone said the dogs were fighting.' A large gentleman strode across the grass towards us.

'It was her fault,' said David, pointing to the girl.

'It wasn't! If you hadn't given Prince your chocolate, Jester wouldn't have tried to get some too. It was his fault, Dad.' The girl pointed to David.

I left them arguing. At least the dogs lived together, and from the sounds of it, fought on a reasonably regular basis. Very relieved, I disappeared for a cigarette.

The Best Puppy class was next, and about fifteen young, exuberant dogs entered the ring with their handlers. The vet explained to all of the owners that he was looking at the condition of the dog, as well as the personality, and it would be these things combined that would help him decide on the winner.

The dogs behaved beautifully, apart from a Cocker Spaniel that got loose and ran around the ring and the dogs in it for ages before she could be caught.

Order resumed, and the vet declared a gorgeous, chunky Shih Tzu as the winner.

Another happy owner, and the ring emptied. Several more classes were held, with rounds of applause and cheering signalling the end of each. I was too busy discussing the habits of a cat that had been brought into the animal centre because he regularly jumped up onto the kitchen cupboard and sprayed urine up the side of the toaster to see the classes, and was trying to convince a couple that as he'd now been neutered, he wouldn't do it any more. They had finally agreed that he was a lovely cat, and they were prepared to offer him a home. With a huge grin, I led them to the office to complete the paperwork.

The last class, The Dog the Judge Would Most Like to Take Home, was about to start and I was in time to watch it. I stood at the edge of the ring and watched as all the dogs paraded around inside. My favourite was a long-haired, black and tan German Shepherd which had been in the puppy class, and a scruffy brown and black wirehaired cross-bred bitch was my second choice.

The vet was moving clockwise around the ring, talking to each of the owners and looking closely at each of the dogs, when another ruckus erupted, this time near the refreshments. Someone screamed, everyone stopped and looked, and my heart jolted as I heard the sound that sent shivers down my spine. I ran around the ring, desperate to get there, but I was too late – Mr Ying, making the awful goose noise he made when he meant business, flapped his way into the ring. His two female companions followed him, adding to the noise.

My heart thumping, my face burning red, I ran into the ring too.

The goose made a beeline for an elderly gent, and the vet valiantly ran in front of the man, with his arms spread wide, but he was no match for the determined bird, who went straight up to him and pecked his ankle. As the vet bent down to stop the bird, Mr Ying pecked his arm, and he cried out in pain. Feeling very sick, I got there just as the goose pecked his shoulder. I lunged and made a grab for his head, but he ducked his long neck down, and wings flapping wildly, rampaged across to the other side of the ring. The girls spread their wings and fluttered after him.

The owners scattered, amid screams of fear and some of laughter, dragging their dogs with them, except for a large gentleman who stood his ground. His dog wasn't as brave, and stood behind his legs. The man crouched, staring at the goose as it approached.

MOVE … for God's sake – bloody move … oh no …

Mr Ying got to him before I did, and as his beak made for the man's crotch, the man grabbed his wing, and grinned as he pulled it up. Mr Ying let out an angry goose noise, and bending his neck round sideways, grabbed the left cheek of the gent's bottom. The man stopped grinning as Mr Ying sank his beak right into the soft flesh. His dog moved round, and stood at the very end of his lead, by his owner's side.

Anna got to them just as I did, and for a split second, we looked at each other. We'd done this before.

'Hello,' she said brightly to the poor man, as she touched his arm. 'Jane is going to get hold of the goose, if you could just bear with us for a couple of seconds.' She smiled sweetly at him.

'Okay.' He said, and tried to smile back at her, but it was more of a grimace.

I smiled too, a false smile, as I wished the ground would open up and swallow me. Never had I had such a big audience when I performed this task.

With a sinking heart, I turned my attention to removing the beak from the man's buttock. The whole dog show had been ruined – by a bloody goose. I'd never hold another event – not ever again.

As I went towards Mr Ying's head, he twisted his beak from side to side, and the man squeaked and jumped a little, before grimacing at Anna again. She looked away, and put her hand over her mouth, but I could see her eyes were crinkled at the corners.

A goose beak has serrated edges, which makes it even more painful for the recipient, and difficult to dislodge, especially when it's half buried in flabby, human flesh, so I knew this was going to hurt both the gentleman and me. I consoled myself that at least my pain was only mental, at the thought of how embarrassing it was for me to have to grab this stranger's arse.

Mr Ying looked at me with one eye. He knew what was coming, and wasn't prepared to let go without a fight. Before setting to the task, I glanced around me. It seemed that the whole world had stopped and was watching in fascination.

This is so embarrassing … I squatted down over the top of the bird and held his wings down with my legs, then got hold of his beak with both hands. It was the usual tussle, and my face burned like mad. I had to prise his beak open with my fingers, bit by bit, and wedge them in his mouth until I was able to break the hold he had. I could distantly hear Anna, nattering away to the man, as my fingers pushed his plump cheek about in order to get a grip on the bird. Suddenly Mr Ying released the bum, and I hung onto him for dear life as I fell over backwards. The vet appeared from nowhere and grabbed him too. As I looked up, the vet stood over me with the goose safely in his arms, so I let the beak go, and heaved a huge sigh of relief.

'It was my fault, really. I shouldn't have grabbed his wing like that. I'm so sorry. I hope he's all right.' The man was apologising to Anna while he rubbed his bottom.

I stood up and brushed some grass out of my hair. *He's apologising for being attacked by our maniac goose* …

Anna took his arm. 'Come and have a cup of tea, sir.' She smiled. 'You don't need to apologise, it wasn't your fault.'

A cup of tea appeared, brought by one of the volunteers, and Anna put in the sugar and stirred. 'Here you are. Would you like a piece of cake? It's the least we can offer you.'

The man took a slice of the proffered cake, and sat, gingerly, on a chair that another volunteer showed him. Anna winked at me, and I went with the vet to put the goose away. The girls were easy to get in, they just followed Mr Ying, even when he was being carried.

I couldn't understand how the geese had escaped, as the door to the shelter was still closed. There was no choice, they'd have to go into the cattery play room, just until everyone had gone.

The vet got straight back into the ring and called for all the dogs to gather again, and much to my amazement, the owners trotted back in for the last class. I was even more shocked to see the gent with the goosed bottom go and stand round about where he had stood before.

There were still three trophies, as the vet hadn't been able to decide who should receive the blank ones. He decided now.

'The first trophy is going to the dog I would most like to take home with me.' He paused for a few seconds, then walked towards an older-looking Labrador cross. The owner blushed as he handed her the trophy, and everyone clapped and cheered.

The vet continued. 'This trophy is going to the second dog I would like to take home with me.' He once again stopped, before heading towards a young Doberman which had a long tail. The man beamed and thanked him.

'The final trophy is going to …' He walked around, and stopped in front of the man who had tackled the goose, then knelt down to the little dog which had remained so calm earlier. 'This little dog.' He stood up, and shook the man's hand vigorously.

I wasn't sure if he genuinely wanted to take the little dog home, or if he did it to make the man feel better. Either way, I didn't care, I was just bloody grateful to him.

To top the afternoon off, the vet joked and laughed with the crowd as he got different people to pull the raffle tickets out of the barrel. And each time he called out a number, he shook the winner's hand, and took time to discuss what prize they wanted.

At last, it was all over, and people left in dribs and drabs. Even though the afternoon had ended well, the memory of the chaos caused by Mr Ying made me resolve never to hold another event again, not after what had just happened.

'Well – what a dog show!' Marie poured us mugs of tea.

I looked at her through a cloud of cigarette smoke. 'Yes; what a bloody dog show. Never again. I doubt anyone will ever want to come here again after that anyway. It'll be the talk of the town. I can just see the headline: GOOSE ATTACKS MEMBER OF THE PUBLIC AT RSPCA DOG SHOW.' I groaned aloud at the thought.

Anna looked at me. 'Don't be daft, woman, they loved it. The man blamed himself too. And look at all the money we've raised.'

I had to admit I was impressed with the three hundred and forty-three pounds that we'd raised, but I was still worried that people wouldn't come again.

'Jane,' said Marie, 'I was at the gate, getting their last coppers out of them as they were going, and loads – yes, loads, of people said it was the best dog show they'd ever been to, and they would definitely be back for the next one. And I'm not just saying that, and you know it.'

'See!' Anna chipped in. 'I told you. People were saying the same to me. They loved it all, especially the goose escaping. It made their day. They thought the vet was great as well, so we'd have to have him as the judge again next time, if he'd be able to do it, that is. The raffle prizes went down very well too, in fact, everything went down well, so stop worrying.' She grinned at me.

'I still don't know how Mr Ying got out. God – I can't believe I had to prise his beak off a man's arse, and in front of all those people.' I cringed again as I relived the incident.

'Imagine if it had been a posh old lady. How bad would you have felt then!' Marie laughed.

I groaned again. 'Oh don't. I don't want to imagine that. It's bad enough.'

'Oh, I forgot to tell you.' Anna leaned forward. 'We have a new volunteer. He's going to come two days a week, just for a couple of hours in the afternoons, and he wants to work with the cats.'

'Brilliant. I'll look forward to meeting him,' I said.

'Oh, you already have,' Anna replied. 'In fact, you know him quite intimately.' She smiled her sweet smile.

'What?' Puzzled, I looked at her. 'Who would I know intimately?'

'Peter – his name is Peter. You know his bum quite well …'

CHAPTER 20

Happy Anniversary

I looked down at the date I'd just written – 7th April – and realised that it was two years to the day since Anna had come to work at the animal centre with me. I put my pen down, and looked out of the office window.

The top branches of the eucalyptus tree that grew directly behind the hedge surrounding my front garden had only just been visible when I first sat and looked out of that window, but now I noticed it had grown by several inches. As I stared at the blue-coloured leaves, which had fascinated me from the first day I'd moved into the cottage, my mind wandered off to recall some of the happy memories of the past two years.

The sudden 'brring-brring' of the phone pulled me out of my reverie.

'Hello, RSPCA, can I help you? You've found a puppy; right. I can give you the number of the dog warden service … What? It was zipped into a shopping bag! Oh my God. Okay, let me take your phone number. I'll get the RSPCA Inspector to call you as soon as possible. Could you keep hold of the bag too? The Inspector may wish to see it or something. Yes? Great. I'll get a message to him immediately. Well, I've got your number, and I'll get him to phone you as soon as he can. Thank you for calling ...'

I sat and frowned at the receiver for a few seconds, pondering the thought that someone was physically capable of putting a puppy into a shopping bag, zipping it up so that there was no escaping from it, taking it to the chosen place, and then dumping it – alone, trapped, and helpless – before walking off.

Sadness filled me. *What sort of ARSEHOLE, could do such a thing ... oh yes ... the same sort of arsehole that dumped the kittens in the cardboard box ...* Shaking my head, I picked up the receiver again and called the RSPCA regional communication centre. There were several of these around the country, and each one was in contact with the group of Inspectors in its own region via radios in their vans. I left a message with Mary, the control room operator.

'Tea, Anna,' I called, as I saw her head bobbing above the low concrete wall of the end dog kennel.

'On my way,' she called back.

'Come on you lot – out for a wee.' I held the office door open and waited for Anna's dogs to go out. Two of them raised their eyelids. 'Come on – wee-wees.' Another eyelid opened, and a back leg slid slowly down the front of the armchair, but within seconds, all eyelids had closed again. 'You *lazy* buggers.' I closed the door to keep the heat in, as it was a bit fresh outside.

'WEE-WEES,' shouted Anna, as she walked through the door. She got more response than me; all eyes opened, and the tip of a tail wagged. As the eyelids began to close again,

Anna looked at them and shook her head. 'You lazy buggers,' she said, and shut the door.

I giggled.

'What are you giggling at?' She stared at me.

'Us lot.'

'Who is us lot?'

'Us, us lot.' I swept my hand around the room. 'I came into the office, said "wee-wees" to the dogs, they didn't move, I swore at them. You, came into the office, said "wee-wees" to the dogs, they didn't move, you swore at them. Identically.'

She laughed. 'Oh dear – I don't know if that's funny or worrying.'

'I know what you mean. Do you realise it's been two years today since we started working together?' I looked at her.

'No! Has it really?' She appeared genuinely shocked.

'Yes, really.' I became serious. 'And they have been the best two years of my working life, thanks to you.' I looked down at the desk and picked up a pen to twiddle, feeling a bit embarrassed at my sudden outpouring.

Anna stopped taking her arm out of her coat sleeve and plonked down onto the chair opposite. She leaned across the desk, and with her free arm, squeezed mine. 'That's a lovely thing to say, thank you.'

'Well, it's the truth.' I looked across at her, and burst out laughing. 'Pull your arm out, woman! You look like a right idiot, sitting with one arm bent backwards like that!'

Anna feigned indignance as she removed her coat. 'Even though you call me names like "right idiot" the feeling is still entirely mutual.' She threw one of her menthol cigarettes at me.

'Why thank you.' I smiled. 'For the mutual feeling, and the cigarette.'

The office door opened and Tony walked in, with a black and white Border Collie puppy under his left arm.

'Oooh,' Anna gasped. 'Let me have him.' She stood up and took the pup, then held it up in front of her face. 'Hello! Aren't you gorgeous?' It licked the tip of her nose. 'Oh – don't you just love the smell of puppy breath.'

Tony laughed. 'No, I don't, and it's a girl.' He looked at me. 'Where's my coffee?'

I grinned at him and got up. 'All right, I'll make it.' I pecked him on the cheek and squeezed past him. 'You can tell Anna about the puppy.'

She was horrified. 'What a bloody bastard! How could anyone do that, especially to a defenceless little puppy.' She was still cuddling the pup, and held her up again. 'How, eh? How could anyone do that to you?' The puppy squirmed, wagged its chubby little tail and licked her cheek. 'Oh – you are just so adorable,' Anna sighed.

Tony went out to his van, and brought back a blue imitation leather shopping bag, which he put on the desk.

'This is the bag she was zipped up in. I've already taken statements from the couple who found her, and a photographer from the local paper is coming out this afternoon to take a photo of the puppy sitting inside it. I want to see if we can find out who dumped her.'

I looked at bag, and pulled the sturdy zip across. There would have been no escape. I shuddered, and pulled the zip open again.

Early the next Thursday morning, I stood in the queue in the newsagents, reading the story about the abandoned puppy, which Anna had nicknamed Zippy. I was chuffed – we had the front page again, with a photo of the puppy standing in the bag, with its front paws leaning against the side of it.

'Whoever did that wants shooting,' the newsagent said, pointing to the photo as he gave me my change. 'I hope you find who did it, love, I really do. Callous – that's what it was – plain callous.'

I smiled at him and nodded. 'Wasn't it? We're hopeful that someone will know something. Fingers crossed.'

It was my day off, but I'd decided to switch the phone's answering machine off early, and stay in the office. I was convinced it wouldn't be long before someone called. Tony joined me for a while. We nattered, while he wrote things in his diary, and I sat on the floor, playing with Zippy.

The phone erupted into life.

I jumped up and grabbed the receiver. 'Hello, RSPCA, can I help you?'

'Hello,' said a quiet, female voice. 'I'm calling about the Border Collie puppy. I think I might know who it belongs to.'

I grinned, and passed the phone to Tony.

After listening for a few moments, I could tell that things weren't going quite according to plan. I stopped playing with Zippy, sat down opposite Tony, and lit two cigarettes. He was frowning, and looking confused, until it seemed the light dawned, and he became angry. He took the woman's name and address and thanked her very much for calling before slowly replacing the receiver.

I waited patiently.

'It would appear that Zippy may not have been dumped in a shopping bag after all. And it would appear that the couple who made statements about how they first spotted the bag, about how they couldn't believe what they saw when they looked inside it, about how they had taken the puppy home and called the RSPCA straight away were lying to their back teeth … as THEY were the owners.' He drew hard on his cigarette.

'Oh.' I didn't know what to say; it was a complete shock.

'I'd better go and pay them another visit.' Tony stood, and slammed his diary shut.

'Tony … you don't know that the woman's got it right. It might be a different puppy she's talking about, so, just take it easy, won't you?' I pulled his arm gently, and forced him to look at me. 'Won't you?' I was really worried; I'd never seen him that angry with a member of the public before.

He put his diary down, put his arms around me, and gave me a reassuring hug. 'I believe her. There was nothing in the newspaper article about the couple who said they'd found the puppy. This woman has just given me their name and address, and said they'd been trying to get rid of a Border Collie puppy for the last few days. She lives next door to them, and had been about to make a complaint about them leaving it outside all the time, but then it disappeared – on the same day as the couple said they'd found just such a puppy in a shopping bag.' He kissed me, and picked up his diary once more. 'They have told me a pack of lies.'

Dread filled me as I watched him stride out through the gate.

Initially, the couple refused to admit what they'd done, but after Tony said it was likely he'd go back to the newspaper with what he'd now been told, the woman broke down and told him the truth. She couldn't tell him why they had concocted the story, because she didn't really know. They both apologised to him, and signed the puppy over to us.

Afterwards, he said he didn't feel good about making the woman cry, but he was satisfied that they regretted what they'd done.

I heaved a sigh of relief; it was finished. Now all we had to do was find Zippy a new home.

Anna adored the puppy, and already it gambolled around her while she did the cleaning, but when eleven o'clock came, and the centre opened to the public, Zippy went into a kennel, where she stayed until lunchtime.

The pup didn't like being shut in on her own, and lay, with her head resting on the side of the red plastic dog bed, whining. Anna checked on her regularly, and pushed treats through the bars.

'When are you going to take her home then?' I stood behind Anna, who had just fed her a bit of sandwich.

'Oh … no. I love all puppies. You know what I'm like.' She turned and walked outside.

I followed her. 'She's meant for you.'

Anna laughed. 'What do you mean, she's meant for me?'

'Well – she's a puppy, and you always take on puppies.'

She laughed again. 'And?'

'And … she's black and white. All of your dogs are black and white,' I offered.

'I can't have another dog though, the car is overflowing already.'

'Ah! You say you *can't* have another dog – not you *don't want* another dog, so that means you want her!' I smiled my smug smile. 'And your car isn't overflowing, there's plenty of room for a little Collie.'

She grinned at me. 'Would you like a cup of tea?'

I grinned back. 'I'd love one.'

The day ended with no offer of a home for the puppy, who was back in the kennel, head on the side of the bed, whining quietly. I felt Anna's pain as she tore herself away and closed the door.

We'd just finished our tea that evening, when I heard bibbing going on outside. I leapt up and ran out.

'Hello! To what do I owe the honour?' I grinned at Marie, who was holding the gate open while her mother reversed into the driveway.

'We've come for her,' Marie whispered. 'Mum can't stand it any more.'

'Ha-ha! I knew it! I must just go and tell Tony.' I ran back indoors.

Anna had the puppy out, and the kettle on, by the time I emerged from the cottage.

Marie handed me a box. 'This is for you.'

I creased my brow, and rested my cigarette on the edge of the ashtray. Whatever it was, was wrapped neatly in newspaper. I looked at Marie as I ripped the paper off to reveal a box of my favourite chocolates.

'Thank you! Erm … what's it for?' I asked.

'Happy two-year anniversary.' Said Anna.

I looked at the chocolates, and swallowed several times, trying to control the lump. After a couple of seconds, it receded. 'Oh wow!' I coughed. 'That's bloody brilliant, but – I haven't got you anything.' I looked at Anna. 'I'll get you something tomorrow.'

Marie held up her hand. 'No need.' She got up, and picked Zippy up from the floor. She held the puppy out to Anna, and raised her eyebrows to me, nodding her head slightly at the same time. 'Ready?' she asked me.

'Ready.' I grinned at her.

'Happy two-year anniversary!' we said together, as Marie plonked Zippy onto her mother's lap.

Anna smiled, and thanked us. 'It was meant to be.'

'Oh, here we go with the fate thing.' Marie laughed.

'It was though. As Jane has already pointed out – she's a puppy, and she's black and white. And – she was brought in on 7th April – the day of our two-year anniversary.' Anna sat back, satisfied with her reasoning.

I looked at her and Marie, and thought about how significantly they'd changed my life. They weren't just work colleagues – they were two of my very best friends. I burst into tears.

Marie jumped up. 'Oh shit, what have we done. Bog roll, we need bog roll.' She flew out to the toilet.

I couldn't help laughing, even though I was crying.

Anna crouched down in front of me, and rested her arms on my legs. 'Come on, you silly old cow, what's up?'

'Oh for God's sake.' I tried to stop, but couldn't.

Marie arrived with reams of toilet roll, and shoved it in my face. 'Come on, woman, pack it in. You'll start me off in a minute.'

I wiped my eyes and apologised. 'They are happy tears, honestly.' I sobbed. 'It's just that, sitting here with you both, now, I realise how much you mean to me. And I'm really glad that you are such a big part of my life. And … thank you … really.'

Anna grabbed some of my toilet roll, wiped her eyes, and blew her nose.

'Oh, come on!' Marie said. 'Don't – you'll start me off too!'

Anna and I looked at each other and laughed.

'Thank Christ for that.' Marie sighed.

I picked up my mug of tea and held it up. 'Here's to us.'

Anna chinked her mug against mine. 'To us.'

Marie chipped in, literally, as a sliver of bone china flew off the rim of her mug. 'Woops. To us.'